YES
FOR
SUCCESS

HOW TO ACHIEVE LIFE HARMONY AND
FULFILLMENT

By
GARY RYAN

Published by Organisations That Matter 2023

First Edition 2023

Copyright © Gary Ryan 2023

All rights reserved. No part of this publication may be reproduced, stored in a retrieval system, or transmitted in any form or by any means, electronic, mechanical, photocopying, recording or otherwise, without the prior written permission from both the copyright owner and publisher.

Disclaimer:

All the information, techniques, skills and concepts contained within this publication are of the nature of general comment only and are not in any way recommended as individual advice. The intent is to offer a variety of information to provide a wider range of choices now and in the future, recognising that we all have widely diverse circumstances and viewpoints. Should any reader choose to use the information contained herein, this is their decision. The author and publishers do not assume any responsibility whatsoever under any condition or circumstance.

The icon image was purchased from Getty Images.

Two images created by Jock MacNeish, Strategic Images.

Book cover design by Louis Salguero, LSUX Design www.lsux.design

Book design and layout by Ravi Ramgati

Edited by Anita Saunders

ISBN: 978-0-6459419-4-4 (pbk – hardcover)
ISBN: 978-0-6459419-0-6 (pbk)
ISBN: 978-0-6459419-2-0 (e-Book PDF)
ISBN: 978-0-6459419-1-3 (epub)
ISBN: 978-0-6459419-3-7 (audio)

Visit: www.yesforsuccess.guru

DEDICATION

Everything I do is inspired by you, Michelle, Liam, Sienna, Callum, Aiden, and Darcy. Your love gives me the energy to back myself every day.

To Eddie and Olga Ryan, thank you for bringing me into this world and giving me opportunities to discover and develop my talents. Without your foresight, steadfastness, love and above all, service, this book would not exist.

To my siblings, your partners, your children, and for many of you, your grandchildren, thank you for your continued support, feedback and faith in what I am doing. Carmel, Jeanette, Terry, Sheryl, John, Rob, Alan, Anne, Brendan, Kelvin, Jennie, Leonie, Rod, Denis, Crystal, Wayne and Lisa, I am honoured to put your names in print and am forever grateful for you being part of my life.

To Denis in particular, you never stop backing me brother, thank you.

To my lifelong friends Mick, Earl and Brendan, you and your wives, Lisa, Heidi and Rose are such incredible people; I can't thank you enough for your love and unconditional, decades-long friendship.

To Kotch, Chief, Dee, Col, Michael, Paulie, Matt, Womble and Rob, the 'brothers' group was a saviour when everything went south in 2020.

To James, Gerry, Jonny and Tommy, the 'regulars' on our rides with Kotch and Dee, we have ridden thousands of kilometres together, each of us having the back of everyone on our motorcycle trips. You have kept me smiling, enjoying life and most of all, sane.

To Mapes and Tania, you have always been there for Michelle and I and we are grateful for your willingness to support us and spend valuable time with us whenever the small windows of opportunity open.

To Greg and Catherine, we never thought we could make new lifelong friends when we met, but thankfully we did and we are so grateful for your presence and support for our entire family, for close to twenty years now.

Finally, to those of you who make the impossible possible through implementing what you learn from this book, and more importantly, what you do with your plan to enable you to live an 'extraordinary, ordinary' life, it is to you I dedicate this book.

PRAISE FOR

Yes For Success: How to Achieve Life Harmony and Fulfillment

"As Gary Ryan's twin, I've had the privilege of experiencing the *Yes For Success* program's earlier versions. Chapter 2's 'Values and Turning Points' exercise reshaped my life. It unearthed my core value, Do the Right Thing, hidden among ten others. My second and third values, Freedom and Responsibility, emerged as often conflicted, revealing a Yin-Yang dynamic in my choices. Reflecting on past pivotal decisions, I realized the program's priceless gift—clarity. *Yes For Success* ignited a harmonious and balanced life I once deemed unattainable. Decisions now flow confidently, anchored in my values. This transformative journey awaits you in these pages. Say *Yes For Success* and change your life."
Denis Ryan, Florida, USA

"*Yes For Success* provides a structured method for intentional reflection, goal and vision setting. It takes a holistic and research-based approach, peppered with personal anecdotes to bring concepts to life. It reflects the realities of our lives and how to stay true to your goals even when difficulties arise to ensure you are celebrating progress."
Sophie Tversky, Business Strategist and Innovation Facilitator, Toronto, Canada

"In this his third book, *Yes For Success,* Gary conversationally shares steps to achieve personal and professional success. Drawing on lived experiences, insights from neuroscience, the arts, nature photography, business and academia, he brings to life a program for Success. For those looking to gain personal insights and realise their potential, I encourage *Yes For Success* to be studied and be a part of your reference library. I wish it was available early in my career."

Malcolm Deery, Managing Director, Designed Culture, Melbourne, Australia

"I did Gary Ryan's original online *Yes For Success* program back in 2013 and found it a very rewarding experience. While I had already done some thinking about what success meant for me, I found his program challenged me to think much more holistically about the success that I wanted for both my personal and professional life. His decision to update that program now, 10 years later, and to write an accompanying book is an inspired move. An incredibly significant shift has happened over those 10 years, most clearly expressed by Simon Sinek who reminded us that people don't buy what we sell, they buy who we are. Gary's book and accompanying program helps us to home in on who we are and what we want to achieve in our lives. But the greatest value of his *Yes For Success* initiative lies in the plan he helps us develop for achieving that. I highly recommend the *Yes For Success* book and the online program. They are a package deal."

Maree Harris, PhD, Director and Mentor, People Empowered, Geelong, Australia

"I love this book for the following reasons—you are getting a practical guide and framework on how to create success; many people can talk at you—few can guide you. Gary Ryan's experience and wisdom is woven through the book based on clear, actionable steps. The *Yes For Success* journey is one of empowerment, action and results."

Alison Wheeler, High Performance Coach, and Author of #1 Amazon Kindle Bestseller, *Living from the Inside Out*, Gold Coast, Australia

PRAISE FOR

"Everybody can be 'good' if they work hard at a young age and dedicate themselves to something they are good at to become a specialist. However, getting from 'good' to 'great' is an entirely different ballgame as it requires you to be consistently 'good' for an extended period. To do that, you will need a great framework, which Gary Ryan's book *Yes For Success* outlines so well. Gary helped me clarify many questions I had early in my career. Completing a version of the *Yes For Success* program in 2011 helped me put context into what I needed to do to advance my career and has continued to provide clarity for my business ToAsia.biz. I highly recommend this book for all professionals, as the tools and techniques you will learn are priceless for all elements of your life."
Alan Wong, Founder and CEO, ToAsia.biz, Hong Kong, China

"*Yes For Success* is a journey inward before embarking outwards towards one's goals. Still, a standout feature of the book is its real-world applicability. The book underscores the importance of individual and shared mental models, emphasizing their role in creating alignment in relationships and ventures. Ryan's insights into the subconscious drivers of our behaviours—the 'iceberg' analogy of our mental models—and the profound effects they can have on our success trajectory are paradigm-shifting. I commend Gary Ryan for the depth to which this book delves into self-discovery, emphasizing the transformative power of understanding one's mindset and the mental models that dictate our daily actions and decisions."
Renata Bernarde, Founder and Host of *The Job Hunting* podcast, Melbourne, Australia

"In 2012, Gary Ryan introduced me to the *Yes For Success* program. It has been a total game changer for me—helping me define my version of success and providing the tension and clarity that pulls me towards it. This book is the distillation of humble but powerful insights, and action-oriented processes that Gary has made into a fine art. There is 'gold' in here for everyone."
David Allt-Graham, General Manager Sales, MAB Corporation, Melbourne, Australia

"I met Gary in 2011 when he hosted an early version of the *Yes For Success* program for the George Alexander Foundation Scholarship at RMIT University, of which I was thankfully a recipient. I remained in touch with Gary through the initial stages of my career and continued to implement the program's principles and techniques, culminating in the establishment of Dean Munro Property, where I own a multi-million-dollar portfolio, and help people purchase their dream property. I am delighted the program is now a book, and recommend you read it and implement its strategies to achieve your version of success."
Dean Munro, Dean Munro Property, Melbourne, Australia

CONTENTS

Dedication iii

Praise for *Yes For Success: How to Achieve Life Harmony and Fulfillment*... v

Introduction 1

Chapter 1: Overcoming Your Fears 5
    The Planning Hierarchy 9

Chapter 2: Background Research 24
    Mental Models 24
    Personal Values 29
    Resistance 36
    Resistance does nothing! 39
    Personal Success Team 40
    Turning Points 43
    Personal Purpose 56

Chapter 3: Core Concept 59
    The Power of Big Questions 71
    Master This System! 74

Chapter 4: Passion 80

Chapter 5: Personal Vision 89

Chapter 6: Present Reality 102

Chapter 7: Identify Strategies 117
    Vital Strategy One: Self-Awareness 121
    Vital Strategy Two: Fitness and Health 125
    Vital Strategy Three: Learn for Success 127
    Vital Strategy Four: Wealth for Life 132
    Vital Strategy Five: Career Options 134
    Vital Strategy Six: Relationships Matter 140
    Six Vital Strategies Summary 143

Chapter 8: Level Two Charts 146
    Level Three Charts 150
    Creating a Ninety-Day Plan 153

Chapter 9: Perform 157

Chapter 10: Review 166

Chapter 11: *Yes For Success* Corporate Program 173

Acknowledgements 175

Bibliography and Resources 177

About the Author 180

Yes For Success: How to Achieve Life Harmony and Fulfillment

INTRODUCTION

Cambridge dictionary definitions:
Extraordinary (adjective): very unusual, special, unexpected, or strange.
Ordinary (adjective): not different or special or unexpected in any way; usual.

Often, at the start of a live workshop, I ask the participants to raise their hand if they are extraordinary. It is rare that anyone raises their hand.

I immediately talk about what happened when my first son, Liam, was born. Michelle had undergone nearly seventeen hours of labour, but Liam was 'stuck'. He couldn't get out. This was a dangerous scenario, so an emergency caesarean section was arranged. Literally within fifteen minutes of the decision being made to surgically remove him from Michelle, Liam was born.

After he had been checked and cleaned, and Michelle had a brief cuddle with him, Liam and I were whisked away to Michelle's room, and left alone. I unexpectedly found myself with our newborn son and I was told it would be about forty-five minutes before Michelle would return to the room. We were alone.

What do I do? I thought to myself.

He was in my arms, and as I looked down at him, all I could see was this incredible human being with his face all scrunched up. He was still covered in vernix caseosa, the white biofilm that covers the skin of babies in the last trimester of pregnancy. I began to talk with him and explained to him why we had chosen his name, who his family was and the extraordinary person he would become. I sang to him for the first time. "Liam Ryan, you are the one, you are the one, Liam Ryan, you are the one for me!"

I ask the audience, "Was Liam extraordinary?"

Every single parent, and most other people, immediately respond, "Yes!"

I then share how I had the same experience with each of Sienna, Callum, Aiden and Darcy, except I knew I would have this time with them because we had planned caesarean sections for each of their births.

Again, I ask, were each of them extraordinary? The response, "Yes!"

I then ask, if every child is born extraordinary, and everyone in this room was once a baby, then wouldn't it be true that you were all born extraordinary, too? And if that is true, why didn't any of you raise your hand and identify yourself as extraordinary?

People give me a perplexed look, and often shrug their shoulders. Most people struggle to offer an obvious reason.

The truth is, well before most of us are adults, the last thing we believe about ourselves is that we are extraordinary. Somewhere between birth and adulthood, we shift from being extraordinary, to ordinary.

What if each of us truly is extraordinary? What if we started to believe that about ourselves?

INTRODUCTION

Please know that when I am saying "extraordinary", I am not saying, "better than everyone else". I am saying, as the dictionary says, "very unusual, special, unexpected, or strange."

I will take any one of those descriptors, any day of the week. I guess having been born the ninth of eleven children, I recognise how lucky I am to exist. Most 'number nines' never get born! So, I have always felt a sense of duty to make my life worthwhile.

I am not perfect. I never was and never will be. I do not want to be perfect. But I do want to 'have a crack at living my version of an extraordinary life' and my hope is that you do, too. No matter what you believe, we only get one go at this life, so it might as well be the best we can make it.

I am not suggesting you must be famous. If that is what you want, then go for it. There is a great deal to be learned from famous people, but there can only be one Oprah, one Richard Branson, one Taylor Swift and one Ed Sheeran.

For the other eight billion of us on this planet, me included, instead of striving to be one of the already existing famous people, what if it is possible to live an 'extraordinary, ordinary life'?

Ordinary in this sense relates to being one of the other eight billion non-famous people. My mind boggles at the possibility of the rest of us being extraordinary in our own way. Surely that would contribute to a decent world to live in!

I believe this is possible. And it is for those of you who share this belief that I have authored this book. Let us become 'extraordinarily ordinary', each in our unique way, together!

I am excited you are reading or listening to this book. My hope is that you join the online program and connect with like-minded people who are striving to help each other on their journey and helping each other be accountable to your own plan.

Finally, this is a 'doing book'. Reading or listening are not enough. You need to commit to completing the exercises, because that is where the gold is for you and for others in your life with whom you share the lessons you learn.

Together, one person at a time, we really can make this world a better place for ourselves and future generations.

Gary Ryan

October 2023

OVERCOMING YOUR FEARS

"Courage is not the absence of fear, but the triumph over it."
Nelson Mandela

Welcome to *Yes For Success*. I am honoured to be your guide on this transformative journey. In this first chapter, we cover the essential elements of the *Yes For Success* program.

Throughout this program, I have carefully crafted eleven chapters that will empower you to create your very own Yes For Success OTM Plan For Personal Success®. Each chapter plays a vital role in shaping your path to success.

Let's begin with Chapter 1, where I lay the foundation and explain the structure of the program. In Chapter 2, I delve into background research, equipping you with the necessary knowledge to excel. Moving forward, Chapter 3 takes centre stage, focusing on a core concept that will illuminate your path to success on multiple levels.

Chapter 4 is dedicated to the exploration of passion—the fuel that propels you forward, and identifying how you will generate the necessary energy to put your plan into action. Chapter 5 encourages you to craft a personal vision, a clear depiction of the future you desire.

As we progress, Chapters 6, prompts introspection. It enables you to understand your present reality and your current place in this world. In Chapter 7 you strategically devise a plan to bridge the gap between your current reality and your personal vision. In this phase, you shall identify the precise strategies required to bring your desired future to fruition.

Advancing further, Chapter 8 dives deeper and unveils the power of identifying detailed, specific actions. Here, you delve into the finer details of your strategies, ensuring crystal clarity in your pursuit of success. This meticulous approach will empower you to overcome any lingering fears or concerns about the future and provide you with certainty and confidence. All the work you have completed to this point comes to fruition.

This chapter highlights the power of being happy and fulfilled while you are taking action to create your future, while also focusing on a future that is acting like a magnet, pulling you towards it. Both are necessary for life harmony and fulfillment. The strategies, tactics and actions you put into practice in this section of the book enable you to be happier in your present because the things you are doing in the present are creating fulfillment 'now'.

This occurs because you know they are taking you towards the definition of success you have defined and refined for yourself. *Yes For Success* is NOT about 'waiting' for success and then becoming happy and fulfilled. It is about helping you to identify the small actions, the small moments, the 'mini successes' that occur along your journey. The more you become aware of these moments of success, the more you become aware of 'happiness moments' in the present, and consequently the more you keep doing the things that are helping your progress, and the more you create the future you desire. This is where you create a deliberate, positive self-reinforcing loop where your happiness and fulfillment in the present increase the probability of creating the future you desire, which reinforces that what you are doing in the present is worthwhile, so you keep doing it.

Chapter 9 emphasises performance and action. This is where your plan comes alive, propelling you forward on your journey towards success. Finally, in Chapter 10, I conclude with a comprehensive summary and review process. It is during this phase that you fine-tune your plan for personal success, ensuring its usefulness as you continue to thrive beyond the current planning cycle.

If you are a leader, Chapter 11 explains how you can apply the *Yes For Success* program within your organisation as a strategy for creating a winning culture. The possibilities are incredible!

Together, we will navigate these chapters, unlocking your true potential and paving the way for a future brimming with success. Let's embark on this empowering voyage with enthusiasm and determination.

Now, let us explore the essence of planning in a simple context. Whenever you embark on a planning endeavour, the first step is to gain absolute clarity regarding the outcomes you seek. Your focus is firmly fixed on what you desire to achieve and the objectives you aim to fulfill.

Moving on to the second step, you must assess your present reality and understand your starting point. This awareness is crucial for charting your path forward.

Steps Three and Four entail identifying the key strategies that will propel you from your current situation towards your envisioned future. In Step Three, you engage in a brainstorming session, determining all the necessary actions to drive progress. Once you have a comprehensive list, it becomes imperative to prioritise these strategies. You must discern the most impactful, high-leverage approaches—the ones that yield significant results with the least effort. These are the strategies that generate a ripple effect, amplifying success in all other areas.

This simple planning process possesses universal applicability. It can be employed for various purposes, whether it be crafting an academic assignment, formulating a project plan at work, developing an organisational roadmap, or serving as the foundation for a personal success plan, or even a surprise party for someone you love.

Allow me to emphasise why we begin with Step One. By starting with a focus on outcomes and the success you desire, you avoid the pitfalls that hinder progress. If you were to commence at Step Two, many individuals would find themselves burdened by reasons why they cannot manifest the future they truly desire. Their present reality would obstruct the formation of a vision or the belief that success can be attained. Hence, starting at Step One is essential for an effective plan.

Even if the aspects of your personal vision outlined in Step One seem outlandish or unattainable, it is vital to record them, nonetheless. By committing them to paper, you grant them validity and importance. After all, why would you invest effort in creating something you do not genuinely desire? Think about that question for a moment.

Even if your aspirations appear far-fetched, embracing them ensures your dedication and provides a clear roadmap for manifestation. This approach maximises your chances of creating the future you yearn for.

The Planning Hierarchy

Figure 1 The Planning Hierarchy

Level One Chart	Level Two Chart	Level Three Chart
Desired Success	Desired Success	Desired Success
Vital Strategies	Vital Actions	Specific Actions
Current Reality	Current Reality	Current Reality
Longer Timeframe	Intermediate Timeframe	Short Timeframe
Clear Direction and Less Specific	Increased Specificity	Highly Specific

If you are listening to the audiobook version, please visit www.orgsthatmatter.com/yfsresources to view the illustration.

The planning hierarchy encompasses three distinct levels. You commence your journey on the left-hand side of the model with what I refer to as the Level One Chart. This serves as your starting point, and from there, you progressively build towards shorter timeframes as you move across the model towards the right. Simultaneously, you delve deeper into the intricacies, adding more and more detail along the right side of the model.

To provide a quick example, one of the **Vital Strategies** I formulated for my personal plan, on my Level One Chart, prior to embarking on Organisations That Matter, was to establish a business. Although slightly more detailed, the initial formulation was not substantial enough to provide a clear roadmap for achieving that desired future.

Figure 2 Level One Chart EXAMPLE

Level One Chart
Desired Success
I will be an awesome husband and father. I will be a successful business-person. I will have helped thousands of people be the best they can be at work and at home. I will be an active member of my community. I will be a great mate. I will be physically, mentally, and spiritually healthy. I will regularly travel to visit my twin brother and his family in the USA.
Vital Strategies
This is one EXAMPLE of a Vital Strategy on the Level One Chart: I will create a consulting business.
Current Reality
I am happily married with three young children and a fourth child due later in the year. I am physically, mentally, and spiritually healthy and have completed two marathons. I have three degrees and I have a great job with corporate experience that is about to end, with a voluntary redundancy available. I have a mortgage and some investments. I have a large number of great friends.
Longer Timeframe
Clear Direction and Less Specific

Recognising the need for greater clarity, I transitioned this vital strategy to a Level Two Chart. This enabled me to create a plan that was specific to that Vital Strategy about my business. As such, I was able to define the business more precisely, outlining aspects such as projected earnings, brand identity and personal profile.

Figure 3 Level Two Chart EXAMPLE

Level Two Chart
Desired Success
My successful consulting business will: Serve at least three billion dollar organisations. Enhance the leadership and culture of organisations so they increase their productivity and are better places to work for leaders and staff and be sought after for leadership development and coaching services. Be a sought after developer and facilitator of undergraduate and graduate student development programs and early career starts to help them create success in the early years of their career.
Vital Actions
This is one EXAMPLE of a Vital Action on the Level Two Chart: I will publish a book.
Current Reality
I have 13 years business experience and have been in a formal leadership role since 1994. I have successfully progressed through the ranks to be a member of the leadership team of a $60 million organisation with 500 staff. I helped create the organisation from a very complex set of previous ownership structures. I have led and mentored leaders to win numerous state and national service excellence awards.. I have three degrees and am currently completing a DBA program.
Intermediate Timeframe
Increased Specificity

Delving into the details, particularly in the 'Current Reality' section, I acknowledged my extensive corporate experience and multiple degrees. However, I had never ventured into the realm of starting my own business. Despite my executive background, starting a business from scratch required a unique set of skills and knowledge.

Among the various actions identified to bridge the gap between my current reality and strategic outcomes, one stood out: to become a published author. Yet, I had never experienced the process of publishing a book myself. Consequently, I needed to elevate this specific action from the Level Two Chart to a Level Three Chart.

At Level Three, I immersed myself in further clarification and specificity. I contemplated the number of book sales I aimed for and considered whether the book would be available in hard copy, soft copy or both formats. Initially, I envisioned a book spanning approximately six hundred pages. However, as my target audience consisted of young professionals, it became evident that a book of such length might dissuade them from engaging fully. Hence, I pondered how to create a book that would cater to their preferences while still providing access to the substantial content contained within those six hundred pages. This led me to develop the idea of an accompanying online course, an avenue through which I could incorporate additional content while ensuring a more manageable reading experience.

Figure 4 Level Three Chart EXAMPLE

Level Three Chart
Desired Success
My book will be available in both physical and ebook versions. I will sell at least 3,000 copies to young professionals, graduating students and senior leaders as a reminder to them of the simple things that matter for a successful career. The book will be available on Amazon and via my website. The book will be published by July 2010.
Specific Actions
Example actions: Recruit a mentor into my Personal Success Team. Research writing courses and attend one if it is highly recommended. Clarify the size of the book. Start writing. Continue to learn and improve.
Current Reality
While I have three degrees and have completed many assignments, including have contributed to a published journal article, I have never written anything for public consumption.
Short Timeframe
Highly Specific

In this way, I adapted and refined my plan, transitioning through the levels of the planning hierarchy, until I established a comprehensive strategy that aligned with my desired future.

Thus, I gained absolute clarity regarding my desired outcome. At the Level Three Chart section, the current reality was crystal clear: Other than contributing to one academic journal article, I had never published anything before for public consumption, and to add to that, I didn't consider myself a particularly skilled writer. Therefore, my task was to identify how to progress from my current reality to the envisioned outcome. Numerous actions unfolded before me, and one action that consistently resurfaced across the levels, from the Level One to the Level Three Charts, was **research**.

I knew I had to commence writing and seek the guidance of a mentor who had traversed this path before. I required someone who comprehended the intricacies of the system. This mentorship was critical to my journey towards the desired success, which involved establishing a blog. I vividly recall my conversation with Futurist, Gihan Perera. When Gihan enquired whether I had started writing, I reluctantly admitted that I had not. His response was direct and profound: "Gary, if you aspire to write a book, you must start writing." He further suggested, "Why not begin with a blog?" Sceptical, I expressed concern that no one would read it.

However, Gihan posed a thought-provoking question, asking if it truly mattered initially if nobody read it. It dawned on me that, indeed, it did not matter, as my ultimate purpose was to publish a book—a realisation that reignited my determination.

In due course, this process led to the formation of an online community in 2013 of over five hundred and fifty individuals and the creation of the OTM Academy which has since been superseded by the various social media follower groups, and specifically the *Yes For Success* Facebook group that is available to people who enrol in the online course. The book, *What Really Matters For Young Professionals! How to Master 15 Practices to Accelerate Your Career* served as a pivotal early offering within the suite of services provided by Organisations That Matter.

OVERCOMING YOUR FEARS

At this juncture, it is worth noting a couple of crucial aspects. As I toiled away, dedicating late nights to my writing, I could discern the profound connection between my efforts on the right-hand side of the model and my overarching personal vision on the left side. I grasped how the two intertwined and were instrumental in shaping the future I aimed to create. This realisation endowed me with tremendous power, enabling me to forge a path towards the success I yearned for, as I could clearly perceive the interdependencies and interconnectedness between my present actions and future aspirations. This level of understanding contributed to the energy required to maintain focus and commit to my actions, specifically, my writing.

Far too often, when individuals experience challenges when actioning their Level Three Charts, they succumb to defeat and give up. They adopt the mindset that their efforts don't really matter. They do this because this is the level that most people plan in their mind. They come up with an idea to lose weight, or start a business, or start a course; heck, it might be as simple as reading a book. Then it gets hard, and they stop.

However, when they possess a plan for personal success and life harmony, they gain a profound understanding of the significance of seemingly small actions and how they directly impact the creation of their vision. They understand the effort they are putting in at this moment is directly related to creating the future they desire. To stop is akin to giving up on their future. So, they keep going, they keep putting in the smart, hard work (I'll explain this concept in Chapter 2).

Now, let us take a moment to revisit the concerns and fears your plan will help you overcome, as well as the desires and aspirations you wish to achieve in your life. Perhaps you worry about your ability to embrace flexibility and seize the opportunities that come your way. You may find yourself in a role where an opportunity presents itself, but due to your own mindset, you lack the necessary flexibility to embrace it.

YES FOR SUCCESS

This concern holds you back, but fear not, for your plan can empower you to overcome these limitations. It can enable you to cultivate the flexibility required to create the success you desire.

Some of you may be plagued by concerns that your past success will come to a halt, leaving you uncertain about the path ahead. Rest assured, your plan serves as a safeguard, ensuring the continuation of your success. It provides the roadmap to sustain and build upon your achievements as you progress forward.

Additionally, many of you may find yourselves uncertain about your chosen career pathway. You question whether it is the right fit for you. As human beings, we possess an innate curiosity and an inclination for exploration. Your plan can be your guiding compass, empowering you to embark on the necessary exploratory journey. It will assist you in gaining clarity and insight into your career pathways, guiding you towards a more fulfilling and aligned trajectory.

In essence, your plan is a powerful tool. It not only addresses your concerns and fears but also opens doors for personal growth, flexibility and self-discovery. Embrace the potential it holds and allow it to illuminate the path towards your desired future.

There are those among you who bear significant concerns regarding working for organisations that truly deserve your unwavering commitment. Perhaps you have endured past experiences where you were treated as nothing more than a faceless number, devoid of recognition as a human being. Naturally, you do not wish to relive such a scenario. Your plan, however, has the power to bring clarity to the type of organisations to which you offer your valuable services. It will equip you with a strategic mindset when it comes to discerning those that may perceive you as merely a number. Furthermore, your plan will instil within you a clear understanding of why you choose to provide your services, for how long and with what ultimate purpose that serves your own needs. It empowers you to navigate your professional journey with confidence and purpose.

For some of you, uncertainty shrouds your future aspirations. You may possess a deep understanding of what you truly want to do or become, but the harsh realities of life can dampen your spirit, leading you to believe that those aspirations are unattainable. Consequently, you find yourself pursuing paths that don't align with your authentic desires. Fear not, for your plan has the potential to infuse your life with your passion to the greatest extent possible. For some fortunate souls, this may even mean earning a living by embracing their passion wholeheartedly. Others will discover how their passion provides the necessary fuel to navigate other aspects of life, allowing them to earn a livelihood that sustains their desired lifestyle.

Amongst you, there are those whose primary concern revolves around achieving a harmonious life balance. The modern world is teeming with busyness, often leading to an imbalance between work and family life, as well as other personal pursuits. Relax, for your plan will restore control and equilibrium to your life. It will guide you in shaping and nurturing the life balance that you truly desire where success is created in all elements of your life.

Embrace the power of your plan, for it holds the key to addressing these concerns and fears. It empowers you to align your work with your values, to pursue your passions, and to create a life that is rich in fulfillment, balance and harmony. Let your plan be the guiding light on your journey towards the personal and professional success you desire.

Amongst you, there are those who bear a weighty concern regarding financial stability. The world we inhabit is undeniably costly, and it is only natural to desire the means to sustain the lifestyle you envision. Be confident, for your plan holds the key to taking the necessary actions that will enable you to afford the future you desire. By understanding the workings of money and planning effectively, you can leverage your resources to your advantage, ensuring that your financial goals are within reach.

Your plan creates certainty and confidence, even when the most extraordinarily unexpected of life events happen. In the first week of the pandemic, 90% of the contracts I had in my business were stopped or paused, indefinitely. Suddenly I had a successful, sustainable business that had ceased to be sustainable, effectively overnight. I had seven mouths to feed. So, how did my plan help? How did it give me certainty and confidence with the actions I was going to take in the most difficult period we had collectively experienced in our lifetimes?

The lessons from Chapter 2, that you will soon be able to apply for yourself, meant that I already knew the mindset I would adopt when the unexpected happened. I was certain and confident because I knew what I would do. Number one I was **certain** I would activate my financial back-up plan. Secondly, I was **certain** I would ask this question, "Okay, what's the opportunity here?"

Did I like the fact that I was in that situation? No.

Life does that. As the saying goes, it throws you a curve ball.

Michelle and I implemented our financial back-up plan, and I got busy answering the question about opportunity. And the opportunity was to write *Disruption Leadership Matters: lessons for leaders from the pandemic*, which went on to become a #1 Amazon Kindle Bestseller and helped to reignite my business.

For some of you, your primary concern revolves around securing a job. You may be apprehensive about the competitive job market and the challenges of finding suitable employment. Artificial intelligence (AI) is here and no doubt you may fear its consequences for your employment. Rest assured, your plan for personal success can guide you in taking the strategic actions required to increase your chances of

OVERCOMING YOUR FEARS

securing the ideal work that aligns with your aspirations. It empowers you to overcome this concern and paves the way for a future brimming with fulfilling career opportunities.

Among your worries lies the concern about living in alignment with your values. You aspire to be an integrated individual, upholding the same values both at home and in the workplace, as well as within your community. You recognise the challenges of maintaining consistency across various domains of life. Your plan, however, can assist you in achieving clarity regarding your values and understanding how to apply them in different contexts. It equips you with the tools to navigate the intricacies of life while remaining steadfast in your principles.

There are those among you who carry a sense of unease about facing a solitary existence. Perhaps the absence of a life partner causes you to worry about the potential loneliness that lies ahead. Fear not, for your plan can empower you to take the necessary steps to expand your social circle, connect with new people, and cultivate the types of relationships that will contribute to your happiness and overall well-being. It will guide you in building meaningful connections and enable you to create a future brimming with success and the lifestyle you desire.

Embrace the power of your plan, for it holds the potential to alleviate these concerns and fears. It empowers you to take charge of your financial well-being, secure rewarding employment, live in alignment with your values and cultivate fulfilling relationships. Let your plan be the compass that guides you towards a future abundant with success, contentment and the realisation of your deepest desires.

Some among you carry a weighty concern about the future, dreading the possibility of looking back one day and regretting the choices not made, the opportunities missed. With your plan, however, such worries can be put to rest. It has the power to ensure that when you reach that future point, you can gaze back and proudly declare, "I gave it my all.

I achieved beyond my wildest dreams, and I wouldn't change a thing." Embracing every challenge along your journey, you can find immense satisfaction in what you have accomplished. Your plan is your guiding light towards this desired outcome.

Another concern that troubles some of you revolves around mindset. You acknowledge that your current mindset has been constraining, akin to being trapped in a fishbowl. You yearn to break free, to venture into new environments, and challenge your limiting beliefs. By doing so, you can open yourself up to greater possibilities and pave the way for the success you crave. Remarkably, I've witnessed individuals transform their lives, even finding life partners, through a shift in mindset. By clarifying their plans and embracing change, they shattered the barriers that once held them back. Their stories exemplify the transformative power of mindset and the capacity to create the life one desires.

Consider this: What would it be worth to you if your plan could conquer your fears and concerns, enabling you to shape the future of your dreams? I urge you to pause and reflect on this question, allowing your answer to surface once more. Many have expressed that such a plan is invaluable, worth many millions. The power it holds to reshape your life and create certainty and confidence about your future is immeasurable. Therefore, I implore you to complete reading this book. Moreover, complete the activities in this book or enrol in the *Yes For Success* Online Course.

By doing so, you give yourself the best possible chance to manifest the success you desire. Your plan empowers you to seize control over what lies within your reach, acknowledging that while certain external factors may be beyond your control—an accident or an economic downturn—you possess more control over your future and success than you might imagine. Believe in your inherent capacity to shape your destiny. And whenever disappointments and seemingly 'bad luck' affect you, always ask, "What control do I have in this situation? How

OVERCOMING YOUR FEARS

have I contributed to this situation? What can I learn?" The alternative is the Poor Me Syndrome. Woe is me! What possible benefit can emerge from that mindset?

Do not underestimate the profound impact your plan can have. It has the potential to transcend limitations, rewrite narratives, and steer you towards a future brimming with accomplishment and fulfillment. So, commit yourself wholeheartedly, for the rewards that await you are nothing short of extraordinary. Full commitment to your aspirations and dreams is key.

Throughout the book you will see the following icon:

This is your prompt to take out your notebook that you have dedicated to completing the exercises associated with the development of your plan for life harmony and fulfillment. If you prefer to use exercise sheets that have been designed for the content, then enrol in the *Yes For Success* Online Course where you have video and audio prompts, transcripts, short quizzes to test your understanding to ensure you are on the right track and the downloadable exercise sheets for you to complete each activity.

I invite you to take a moment, take out your notebook for the first time and pause to complete the exercise.

Engage in the exercise and ponder: What does success truly look like to you? How would you define it? Set aside a few minutes to complete this contemplation: What is your personal view of success?

Welcome back, and congratulations on undertaking this short yet meaningful activity. Throughout the years, countless individuals have shared with me that success is a subjective concept, defined by everyone according to their unique perspective. It is a personal journey. There exists no universal definition of success, despite the narrow societal portrayal propagated by the media, fixated on wealth and prestigious titles. This portrayal represents an exceedingly limited view of what true success encompasses.

Time and time again, people like yourself have expressed that success is intrinsically linked to happiness. Happiness and success are intertwined. Our pursuit of happiness and the level of joy we experience in our lives, both presently and in the future, form integral components of your personal success.

Consider this: To lead others effectively, you must first learn to lead yourself. A powerful avenue for self-leadership is the creation of your own plan for personal success. This plan is exclusively tailored to you, unveiling the precise actions you need to take to navigate the path to success. By embarking on this journey, you not only enhance your own leadership capabilities but also become an inspiration to others. People will naturally gravitate towards you, eager to listen and follow your lead, captivated by the tangible evidence of your ability to craft the success you desire, all through the power of your written plan.

Let us delve into the remarkable potency of a written plan. Dr David Ingvar, a distinguished Swedish neurologist, conducted groundbreaking research known as 'memories of the future'. His findings revealed that when we document future-focused ideas or plans, outlining how we intend to manifest them, we create a memory of the future. Like our recollections of the past, this practice imbues clarity and focus upon the future we ardently seek. Even if you don't revisit your written plan for an extended period, when you eventually reflect upon your actions over time, you will realise, with astonishment, that you have accomplished the very things you once inscribed. "Hey," you'll exclaim, as you rediscover the aspirations you had penned down. "I actually did that! I brought this into fruition!" By aligning your actions with the vision encapsulated within your written plan, you manifest that desired future, transforming it from a mere aspiration into a vivid reality.

Writing down your plan has transformative power. It becomes a testament to your commitment, propelling you forward, and serving as a compass guiding your actions. Embrace this practice, for it has the potential to reshape your life in awe-inspiring ways.

Even when obstacles arise, impeding your progress and acting as roadblocks on your journey, your plan will provide you with unwavering clarity. It will equip you with the ability to take decisive action, a crucial aspect we will delve into further when we explore Chapter 9: Perform. With this newfound clarity, you will confidently embark on the necessary actions required to shape the future you desire. The act of committing your plan to paper, enhancing its focus and adding more intricate details holds an astonishing power. Dr David Ingvar's research confirms this, revealing the extraordinary efficacy of written plans in propelling individuals towards action and facilitating the creation of your desired success.

Congratulations, we have reached the conclusion of Chapter 1. What lies ahead? Chapter 2: Background Research.

You've made remarkable progress thus far, and I encourage you to proceed to Chapter 2 at your earliest convenience. I eagerly anticipate our collaboration in this next phase. Remember, the key to continuous growth lies in embracing a lifelong commitment to learning and striving to become the best version of yourself.

BACKGROUND RESEARCH

"Research is formalized curiosity. It is poking and prying with a purpose."

Zora Neale

In this chapter, our focus will be on self-discovery because understanding yourself is crucial in shaping the future you aspire to achieve.

We will delve into various aspects of self-awareness, starting with your mindset and comprehending your mental models. Next, we will explore your values and help you uncover your personal set of values. Identifying your personal success team will also be a significant part of this chapter. Additionally, we'll guide you in recognising pivotal moments from your past and defining your personal purpose.

To proceed, please be ready to complete the extensive activities. Have your notebook ready.

Mental Models

Let's begin by discussing mental models. Your mindset plays a crucial role in creating success; in fact, it holds immense power and can either propel you towards success or hinder your progress. Through my work with countless individuals, I have discovered that success often originates from one's mindset.

BACKGROUND RESEARCH

Mental models are your theories about how the world works. They are formed through your life experience. Your upbringing, family life, education, religious, humanistic or atheist beliefs, national cultures, your travel experiences, your work experiences, your experiences of leaders and much, much more.

For most people, your mental models are subconscious. You have them, and while they directly influence your behaviour, you are not aware of how they are affecting you. Much like an iceberg, where your behaviour sits above the waterline, visible and recordable to the world, your mental models sit below the water, invisible to the naked eye.

Raising your iceberg out of the water enables you to become aware of your mental models. Through my work with countless individuals, I have discovered that success originates from one's mental models. Everything starts with your mindset.

For instance, I once had a participant in a program who shared her experiences of relationship breakdowns. Despite her strong desire to find a lifelong partner, she held certain beliefs about how she should go about meeting someone. Specifically, she firmly believed that online dating services were not a viable means to find a lifelong partner. Her mental model represented a theory because mental models are essentially theories about how we perceive the world and what we believe to be true or false.

In an enlightening session during our face-to-face program, she revealed to me that this mental model might be holding her back from meeting potential partners. She decided to challenge her theory by conducting some research. As we progress through the upcoming chapters, you will notice that research is often a critical step in creating your desired success.

Research allows us to expand our understanding and challenge our existing beliefs. It empowers us to take informed actions aligned with our aspirations.

Remember, understanding and reshaping your mental models are key elements in your journey towards success. So, let's get started on this transformative process together.

In this example, she embarked on her research journey by seeking recommendations from friends who had used online dating services. She wanted to know which platforms they found to be the most reliable and effective. With their input, she devised a strategy and implemented it. Remarkably, it was the third person she met through this process whom she fell in love with, and within a span of approximately eighteen months, they tied the knot in a picturesque island wedding ceremony in the Pacific. This joyful outcome delighted not only her but also her family and, of course, her new lifelong partner. It all stemmed from her willingness to shift her mental models. Years later, she and her life partner are the proud parents of two extraordinary children. Now, that's a story of triumph in the realm of relationships!

Mental models influence various aspects of our lives. They shape our perspectives on finances, career success and other domains. These models are present everywhere, and their impact is significant. Henry Ford's powerful quote "If you think you can or if you think you can't, you're right either way" encapsulates the essence of mental models. They have the power to validate or invalidate our beliefs, ultimately determining our outcomes.

Think of mental models as directors for the video camera of our perception. Our eyes and ears serve as the cameras, while our mind directs them. Mental models exert great influence, as they are rooted in our beliefs and shaped by our upbringing and life experiences. They guide our focus, determining what we see and what remains unnoticed.

Their influence can be so profound that they may lead individuals to harbour racist beliefs, associating negativity or positivity solely with specific races or religions.

We often use our mental models to confirm pre-existing beliefs, selectively accepting data that aligns with our views while dismissing or disregarding contrary evidence. Our assumptions and beliefs, rooted in these mental models, can even lead us to fabricate or insert information that doesn't actually exist.

Understanding the power and impact of mental models is crucial as we embark on this transformative journey of self-discovery and personal growth. By examining and reshaping our mental models, we gain the ability to perceive the world through new lenses, unlocking greater potential for success and fulfillment.

What truly matters when it comes to mental models is not whether they are right or wrong, but whether they are useful in helping us create the life balance and success we desire.

Consider a simple example: I have a pen in my hand right now. If I were to throw it up in the air, the theory suggests that what goes up must come down. However, if I were to repeat the same action in space, outside a spaceship, the pen would continue to float away. The theory of gravity that governs objects on Earth does not apply in the weightlessness of space. Once again, it is not about the absolute correctness of our mental models, it is about their utility in our pursuit of a fulfilling and successful life.

Furthermore, shared mental models hold even greater power. That is why engaging in this program with your life partner can be immensely valuable. Discussing your shared theories and beliefs about success will strengthen your alignment and synergy. I have personally experienced the strength of shared mental models during challenging times in my entrepreneurial journey. When there was no income flowing into my business, my wife, Michelle, shared the same mental models and theories about how we would achieve success. Her unwavering belief in our shared vision alleviated stress and propelled us forward. Imagine the difference it would have made if we had conflicting theories during those high-pressure periods. Therefore, remember that your mental models possess tremendous influence, especially when they are shared. If you do not have a life partner, seek support from a family member or close friend who can provide similar encouragement and solidarity.

Your mental models manifest themselves through your own words or the words of others. When people utter phrases like "I can't", "Everyone knows you should do this", "The boss thinks" or "Someone else thinks that" they are expressing their theories about other individuals, situations or themselves. Our mental models are evident in our actions and inactions. They form the behavioural foundation of our beliefs. To create the success you desire, it is crucial for you to become more aware of your mental models and to cultivate a heightened consciousness of your mindset. You must be willing to shift your mindset and embrace new mental models if you discover that they will serve you better in achieving the success you desire.

According to Chris Argyris, a renowned researcher from Harvard University, true learning occurs only when we change or modify our mental models. Now, I won't claim that shifting or changing our mental models is an easy task; if it were, we wouldn't need to embark on this program. However, I will emphasise that it is essential to remain open to the notion that oftentimes, we are the ones holding ourselves back.

It is your mental models, your mindset, that impedes your progress in creating the success you desire, rather than external factors. So, I invite you to pause now and jot down some notes about your mental models regarding personal success. Reflect on your response to the question in Chapter 1 about success. What theories do you notice? Spend a few

BACKGROUND RESEARCH

moments reflecting on this question, capturing three or four bullet points.

Welcome back! Although I didn't explicitly mention 'mental models' or 'mindset' in Chapter 1, your answers to the question 'What is your personal view of success?' reflect your mental models on this subject. It would be fascinating to see if your mental models remain consistent between Chapters 1 and 2 or if they have already begun to evolve.

Personal Values

Now let's talk about values. Our values are evident in our actions across all the different roles we play in life. What do I mean by life roles? Personally, I am a son, a brother, a father, a husband, a businessman, an entrepreneur, a director, a board member, a community member, a volunteer for junior sport, a supporter, a mate and the roles continue. Just like you, I have numerous roles throughout my life.

The question and challenge arise: Do you aspire to be a person of consistency across all your life roles? Of course, you will behave differently in your interactions with your parents compared to your best friends, but can you find consistency in how you behave within these distinct roles based on your values?

Or perhaps you are unaware of your values, making it difficult for you to maintain consistency. Our values play a crucial role, and many people fail to realise that their mental models can be so powerful that they can override their values. Let me give you a simple example. Imagine a person who holds the mental model that, as a senior leader or boss in an organisation, they must have all the answers. They also value honesty and integrity. However, when a team member challenges them with a question they don't know the answer to, their mental model kicks in, telling them that admitting ignorance will result in a loss of face and status. So, to save face, they make up an answer, even though it contradicts their value of honesty and integrity.

This is what happens when individuals are not aware of how these various factors interplay. That's why, if you truly want to create the success you desire, you must gain clarity on your mental models and values and understand how they work together. This will enable you to maintain consistency both in achieving your goals and across all aspects of your life.

Now, I want to acknowledge the remarkable woman named Michele Hunt, from whom I learned the activity I'm about to guide you through to help you discover your personal values. I first encountered this exercise from Michele back in 2000, and I have continued to utilise it ever since. You can learn more about Michele and her incredible journey at www.DreamMakers.org. Her story is truly captivating, particularly her experiences growing up as the only African American family on military army bases in the southern states of the United States during the late 1950s and early 1960s. Her journey unfolds to reveal her role as an advisor to President Clinton in the 1990s and how she eventually established her own business, assisting individuals and organisations in understanding the significance of values.

Now, take a moment to gather four Post-it Notes or tear a sheet of paper into four equal pieces. Pause if you need to. You now have your four Post-it Notes or four torn pieces of paper. This activity is designed to elicit a range of valid responses, and any response you have is valid.

BACKGROUND RESEARCH

Its purpose is to help you determine whether what you write down on these pieces of paper aligns with your core values.

Write down one core value on each of the four Post-it Notes or pieces of paper. If you're unsure about what a core value is, it's usually the opposite of something in life that greatly upsets you. For instance, if being lied to deeply upsets you and you discover clear evidence of someone outright lying, it triggers a strong emotional reaction. In this case, the opposite of lying would be a value like honesty or integrity. Similarly, if you feel a strong urge to protect and fight for your family when they are threatened, family becomes an example of a core value.

Consider what your three or four values might be. They don't have to be single words; they can be statements. It doesn't matter if others don't fully comprehend what you write down. Think about the things that upset you the most and identify their opposites, as those are likely to be your values.

Take a moment to pause and reflect on what you believe your four core values are. Write them down now.

Welcome back! Excellent work. You now have your four core values in front of you. I'd like you to place all four core values in your preferred hand, whether that's your right hand or your left hand. Hold them securely in your hand, please.

Great job! Life can present us with significant challenges. I want you to set aside one of your core values. Take one of them and crumple it up, so you can still firmly hold on to the other three. Identify which of your core values is the least important to you at this moment, the one you could temporarily set aside while maintaining a firm grasp on the remaining three.

Take a moment to do that now. You should now be firmly holding on to three core values while one remains crumpled and set aside. I'm crumpling up one as well. Now, I want you to repeat the process.

Among the three core values that you still have in your preferred hand, choose which one you would set aside next, allowing you to firmly hold on to the other two. Crumple that one up as well, leaving you with two core values that you continue to firmly hold.

That concludes the exercise. Once again, all responses are valid. Our aim is simply to explore whether what you initially wrote down as your four core values truly align with your deepest values. In face-to-face programs, I've witnessed a wide range of reactions to this activity. Many participants have expressed feelings such as, "Gary, when you asked me to crumple up that first value and set it aside, it felt as if you were asking me to amputate my left arm. It made me feel disconnected and incomplete." If you've experienced a similar reaction, it signifies that everything you wrote down on those four pieces of paper or Post-it Notes resembles core values, and that realisation is incredibly powerful.

Others have shared different perspectives, saying, "You know what, Gary? To complete the activity, I crumpled up a value and put it down. However, I integrated the meaning of that value into one of the ones I still had in my hand. So, in reality, I didn't truly discard it."

Once again, if that's your reaction, it means you have discovered that what you wrote down are indeed core values.

This kind of reaction reveals something else as well—it highlights the fact that our understanding of our values deepens over time. Through the challenges we face and the experiences we go through in life, we gain a greater insight into our values. The reaction of embedding the meaning into another value is an example of that process.

Some individuals have shared a different experience, saying, "You know what, I actually found it quite easy. In fact, out of the two values in my hand, I know that one of them is the core, the foundation from which everything else stems." If that's the case for you, perhaps you

BACKGROUND RESEARCH

have only one core value, and the others are important values but not at the same foundational level. And that's perfectly fine. This activity has helped you recognise that what you have written down are more like core values than not.

Now, people often ask me, "Do you really have to prioritise your values, Gary?" Well, the answer is yes. You may have come across this concept if you've read my book, *What Really Matters for Young Professionals: How to Master 15 Practices to Accelerate Your Career*. In the book, I recount a personal story about a crucial moment in my life. My wife, Michelle, was ten weeks pregnant with our third child. She had previously experienced two miscarriages, both occurring around the eleventh week. Unfortunately, I was present for one but away due to work commitments during the other.

I was aware of the emotional toll those miscarriages had taken on Michelle. It was a Thursday afternoon at midday when I received a call from her. Just one hour later, at one p.m., I was supposed to be at a different location, facilitating a workshop for thirty-two people. Michelle said to me, "Gary, I think I'm losing the baby. I'm going straight to the hospital. Can you meet me there, please?"

In that moment, my values of family and service clashed. I couldn't physically be at the hospital, which was in the city, and at the other location, which was 20 kilometres away from the city, simultaneously. It's simply not possible to be in two separate locations at the same time.

Furthermore, considering my wife's history in this particular situation, I understood that she didn't need me to respond with something like, "Look, Michelle, I'll get back to you in a few minutes. Let me just check my calendar." That kind of response wasn't what she needed in that moment. She needed immediate support.

So, in that instance, I made a decision. I said, "Yes, I'll get there as quickly as possible." At that moment of saying 'yes', I didn't even know if I could find someone else to cover for me in the workshop, and I wasn't sure if I could contact the client to inform them of my absence. Once I reached the hospital, my phone would be turned off (unlike today, phones had to be turned off in hospital back then due to them interfering with equipment), and I would be out of range, making me unreachable. By saying 'yes' to Michelle, I was taking a risk with my commitment to service.

There was a possibility that at one p.m. that afternoon, there would be thirty-two staff members sitting in a room, expecting a workshop to take place, but no facilitator would show up. This meant there was a potential risk to my reputation and personal brand, at least temporarily, until the staff found out what had occurred. Luckily, I managed to arrange for another team member to cover for me. Although he was only familiar with 50% of the content, he explained the situation to the participants, and later we arranged for me to return and complete the program. So, everything worked out fine. However, in that moment, when I was speaking with my wife, Michelle, my commitment to service was overridden by my dedication to my family. As for the miscarriage, it never happened. The event was just a 'scare'. The baby, Callum, is now a healthy eighteen-year-old and an awesome stage performer.

Now, let's consider a different scenario. My daughter approached me on a Sunday night, saying, "Dad, tomorrow I have a demonstration of our school aerobics, and I'd really, really love for you to be there. It's at two p.m. Can you come along?" I responded, "How long have you known about this?" She replied, "Oh, a few weeks." I said to Sienna, "This is the first time I'm hearing about it. Tomorrow, I have a client that I'll be with the entire day." She then asked, "Well, can't you come anyway, Dad?"

I gently replied, "Sorry, Miss, I can't come. I'm not able to make it." To my surprise, she burst out, "You don't love me!" When daughters say such things to their fathers, it's undoubtedly unfair. In that moment,

BACKGROUND RESEARCH

my commitment to service triumphed over my devotion to family. However, one could argue that my service value, which involves earning money for my family, is also in service of my family value. Yet, from my daughter's perspective, it seemed that my service value overshadowed my family value. Understanding your values empowers you to make the right decisions at the right time, driven by the right reasons for yourself. Fortunately, I saw her perform many times and was heavily involved with her sport activities. So, I didn't take her short-term disappointment to heart.

Values guide us in making the right decisions at the right time for the right reasons. They serve as our compass in varying circumstances and situations. The challenge lies in not knowing our values, as it hinders us from making these types of decisions.

As Ralph Waldo Emerson famously said, "What you do speaks so loudly I cannot hear a word you say." Our actions speak volumes and reflect our true values. In your notebook, I encourage you to create a template with two columns and four rows. List your values in the left-hand column. Then, write down two behavioural statements for each value. By transforming your values, often expressed as high-level words like 'service', 'family' or 'integrity', into clear behavioural statements, you bring them to life in a tangible way.

I have an example here to illustrate the value of integrity. The corresponding behavioural statements are as follows: "I will do what I say. I will do to the best of my ability. If I make a mistake, I will admit it and do my best to fix it as soon as possible." These two clear behavioural statements exemplify the essence of integrity. Understanding our values at the behavioural level grants them immense power.

I'd like you to draft your own behavioural statements for your values. Remember, these statements should be action-oriented sentences, using phrases like 'I will'. Verbs such as 'do' or 'make' are crucial in describing behaviours aligned with your values. Please pause here and complete this activity.

Well done! Great work. Crafting these statements may take some time, but their impact is truly remarkable. As we explored in Chapter 1, writing down these statements helps internalise their meaning, increasing the likelihood of consistency between your actions and words. This consistency is crucial for your success across all aspects of your life—relationships, health, work, studies and more.

The next topic we will discuss is 'Resistance'.

Resistance

Imagine you are standing on one of our beaches here in Australia. The 'back beaches', as they are called in my home state Victoria, are where the surfers go because of the big waves. They are called 'back beaches' because the major city, Melbourne, is on a bay which is relatively calm. The 'back beaches' are at least 90 kilometres from the city, face the open ocean and have massive waves.

So, imagine you are standing on the shore of one of our back beaches. Waves roll in and crash on the beach. There are normally three to four 'sets' of waves rolling in at any one time. Picture a yacht. Your yacht, that is anchored just beyond the sets of waves where they start to roll into shore. Your yacht contains your definition of life harmony and success. To reach your yacht, there is only one way you can get to it.

You must swim. Let's assume you are a competent swimmer (never try this if you aren't a competent swimmer. In fact, even if you are a great swimmer, don't try this because many good swimmers have drowned swimming in these waters!).

While you swim towards your yacht, what are the big waves doing to you?

Correct; they are pushing you back to shore. They are stopping you from getting to your yacht.

This is exactly what 'Resistance' is.

Resistance exists as a force whose sole purpose is to stop success. What's amazing about Resistance is that it never sleeps. It can come to you in your dreams. If you've ever had something important in your life that you've been working towards, and you've had a crazy bad dream the night before you've been going to go and do it, well, that's Resistance.

How does Resistance know to come to you in your sleep?

Resistance has amazing intelligence and cunning. It is at least as intelligent and cunning as you are. It can morph into many forms. Have you ever had a situation where the people who love you, when you tell them what you're going to do, say things like, "Are you crazy, you can't do that!"?

"What are you going to do for money?"

"How are you going to survive?"

"Do you know how hard it is?"

Have you ever had people who love you say things like that?

That's Resistance morphing into the form of people who love you, and it will use logic and your present reality against you.

It will use facts against you. Resistance will tell you about all the things and all the reasons why you can't do whatever it is that you're aiming to do, and its fuel is fear.

Its fear is not the fear of failure. It is the fear of success, and the fitness industry knows this to be true. You think of people, and it might have even been you, who have been on a weight loss program. They successfully get to lose the 5 kg or whatever it is that they're aiming to lose, and then six months later, you see them, and what's happened, they've put the 5 kg back on, and often added some extra on as well!

Now, what that is, is that the people are actually fearful of the success of keeping that weight off over time and what that's going do for their life.

So, Resistance gets strong. In fact, as you get close to success, it gets stronger.

Now, the important thing is, Resistance is in you, but it isn't you. I know that's going to sound a little bit crazy.

It is in you, but it isn't you, and as I have already mentioned, it feeds off the fear of others, and it grows in strength the closer you get to success.

Let me illustrate this point. When I did my writing course with Dale Beaumont to enable me to write my book *What Really Matters For Young Professionals!* I learned from him that 95% of books never get published. They get written but never published.

Why? Because the people who write them know that as soon as they publish their book, it's going to get judged, just as my books have been judged. Some people are going to say it's great, and some people are going to say it's not great.

Even JK Rowling has had people say that her Harry Potter book series is not great. So, some people get so fearful about the negative feedback they might get that they stop and don't publish their book. You might find that Resistance is present in the virtual room right now!

You might find that your mind is going, "This is just a load of crap! What's Gary going on about? Resistance isn't real."

It is real, and you know it's real because you have experienced it already. What's amazing about Resistance is that it lies idle when what you are doing is taking you **away** from success.

So, when you're watching reality TV (the tenth show in a row) and you've got other things that you could be doing during that time, and a little voice goes off in your head and says, "Hey, get up. You should be doing something else, something worthwhile."

Resistance does nothing!

And if you've ever been lying on a couch, have you ever noticed how heavy your legs feel when you go to get off that couch when you know you should have been doing something else? Your body feels so heavy! That's just the weight of Resistance, just loving sitting on top of you while you're **not** doing actions that are taking you towards success.

Now, Resistance is a mighty foe, but the most important thing is that it can be defeated and that you are defeating it every time you continue to read this book and complete each exercise.

Every time you complete a chapter, you are defeating Resistance. More importantly, every time you take an action that you write down in your plan to help you continue to create more success, you are defeating Resistance.

I've known about this concept for twenty years, and I must fight Resistance daily. So, I'm sorry to tell you that folks! I'm sorry to tell you that you've got to learn to fight this every day, but it's true, and the more that you can defeat Resistance, and the more evidence that you've got that you can defeat Resistance, the more you're able to continue to defeat it going forward into the future.

And on the odd occasion when Resistance defeats you, that's okay. You say to yourself, *"All right, that's cool. I understand it is a mighty foe, and sometimes it will beat me, but I will beat it tomorrow!"*

And you set yourself up, and you take it on, and you defeat it. Suppose you choose to enrol in the online program. In that case, you'll receive regular reminders to help you defeat Resistance and because of how mighty a foe it is, you will need periodic reminders to overcome it on your journey. Fortunately for you, it now has a name. **Resistance**.

Now that it has a label, you can recognise it and possess the tools to confront it. This newfound awareness empowers you to conquer Resistance daily, paving the way for achieving your desired success.

Personal Success Team

Let's shift our focus to your Personal Success Team. As you embark on your journey to success, it's important to recognise that we all need the support of others. In a somewhat self-centred notion, if you aspire to create success for yourself, you must actively recruit people into your life who will help you achieve your fullest potential.

Within your life, there are already individuals who are contributing to your progress. Consider your life partner, if you have one, or your parents—who may or may not still be with you. In most cases, they have played a significant role in supporting your development. You may also have critical friends, teachers and mentors—various people who are present in your life and provide assistance. Now, it's crucial for you to identify your critical personal success team members—the individuals who will empower you to achieve the success you desire.

BACKGROUND RESEARCH

Let me demonstrate the power of a Personal Success Team. When I completed my first marathon, the New York Marathon in November 2006, and when I published *Disruption Leadership Matters: lessons for leaders from the pandemic* in November 2021, I was extremely happy and proud. At first glance, these achievements may appear to be the result of my individual efforts. I had to write every word of the book and run every step of the 42.195-kilometre marathon. However, behind both accomplishments, there were numerous individuals who educated, mentored and supported me along the way. My wife, Michelle, and my children were there for me. Maree Harris PhD provided unwavering support for the book project, as well as the editors who fine-tuned my work and the experts who taught me running techniques. They guided me on nutrition and hydration strategies throughout my training and during the race. These are the people who enabled me to create those successes.

Remember, success is not achieved in isolation. It thrives on collaboration, guidance and through the support of your personal success team.

So, when we examine our individual successes, it becomes apparent that none of them are truly achieved in isolation. They are the outcome of the support and assistance we receive from others. Therefore, I argue that individual success is not purely individual—it is a collective effort.

It is time to take out your notebook and reflect on the individuals who could form part of your personal success team. They may include family members or mentors. Speaking of mentors, my simple definition for them is wise people. They are often older than you, although age is not a prerequisite. Mentors possess wisdom and may specialise in specific fields. For instance, you might have a fitness coach or financial advisors. Critical friends are also valuable team members who keep you grounded and never let your ego inflate. Additionally, if you have colleagues or team members at work, they can contribute to your personal success team. Take a moment to jot down the names of individuals who could be part of your team, understanding that the team itself may not physically come together.

Individually, you collaborate with these team members, working together to support and uplift one another. There is a concept called 'enlightened self-interest' that underpins the creation of your personal success team. It means that by striving to be the best version of yourself, you are better equipped to serve and support others. Therefore, forming a personal success team is not a selfish act but a means to recruit people who will help you reach your highest potential. In turn, you can then use your abilities to benefit others and be the best version of yourself for them.

Please take a moment to note down the members of your Personal Success Team, now.

Great job, well done. This exercise can be truly eye-opening for many individuals as they discover areas where they may need assistance. It's possible that you might identify gaps in your personal success team, such as needing support in areas like health and fitness or finance. These roles may not have names next to them yet, but you recognise the need to fill them. These insights will guide you in developing the necessary actions and strategies to achieve the success you desire.

Let's consider the flipside of your Personal Success Team. In your notebook, I want you to note down whose Personal Success Team you are on. My own list includes multiple individuals. For instance, if you have a life partner, see yourself as a member of their Personal Success Team. Currently, my wife, Michelle, is taking on new responsibilities at work, and I am part of her team, supporting her in achieving this personal milestone.

Your list could include family members, children, colleagues or critical friends. If you hold a leadership role in an organisation or team, I will argue that your team members are individuals for whom you are part of their success team, particularly in terms of their career growth.

If you haven't completed this activity yet, I encourage you to 'pause' now and reflect on the individuals whose success teams you are a part of.

Turning Points

Welcome back! Once again, you've done a fantastic job. Let's keep the momentum going. Now, let's shift your focus to turning points. There are certain events in life that hold such significance that they shape your very being.

Let me reiterate: Some life events are incredibly profound, shaping who we are and serving as pivotal moments or 'Turning Points'. These turning points provide us with a deep understanding of our identity and the reasons behind our current situation.

Please prepare to record three to six turning points in your notebook. These can be events, choices or advice that have had such a profound impact on your life that you sincerely believe, had they not occurred, you wouldn't be here, participating in this program. They might have influenced the role you hold at work or even the person you have chosen as your life partner if you indeed have one. These turning points can emerge from any stage of your life, and your level of control over them may have varied at different times.

Allow me to share a few examples: In 1974, when I first attended primary school, being a twin presented a unique situation. The school advised my parents that they wanted my twin brother, Denis, and me to be placed in the same class. Initially, the school had three prep classes, making it easy for us to be separated.

My parents held the belief that my twin brother, Denis, and I should be separated at school, whereas the school had a different perspective. They wanted us to remain together. So, my parents made a decision. They wanted us to enjoy the special bond of being twins, but they also wanted us to develop independence. As a result, we were placed in separate classes.

During the initial three weeks of my schooling experience, a challenging situation unfolded. At the start of each class, I would find myself overcome with longing for my twin brother. I would cry and yearn to be with him. In response, I would rush out of my assigned class, retrieve my bag, and embark on a 2-kilometre run home, along two busy main roads. When I reached home, my mother would discover me hiding behind the couch. She would coax me out and then walk me back to school. It's important to note that my mother didn't drive, so this routine repeated itself every day for three weeks. Just imagine the immense pressure I was unintentionally placing on my parents, particularly my mother, to have us placed in the same classroom. The school, in turn, would point to these struggles as proof that we should have been kept together.

After three weeks, I came to a realisation. If I continued running home each day, I would have to endure an additional 4 kilometres of walking—2 kilometres back to school and another 2 kilometres back home at the end of the day.

BACKGROUND RESEARCH

Indeed, as a five-year-old, I was quite an example of fitness! Who would know that thirty years later all that running would prepare me for marathon running! At the time, however, I soon realised that the circumstances surrounding me were unchangeable. With this understanding, I made the conscious decision to go with the flow and little did I know that this mindset would shape my journey in significant ways. I remained separated from Denis and got on with my education.

Five years later, at the age of ten, my parents sat Denis and me down for an important discussion. They wanted to know our preferences for secondary school. Denis, influenced by our older brothers' footsteps, expressed his desire to attend the local technical school. It was a path well trodden by our siblings, and he was enticed by the prospect of a school without homework. Additionally, he aspired to follow the family tradition by becoming a tradesman, just like our brothers and father.

On the contrary, I felt a sense of inadequacy, as if I possessed ten thumbs. Despite performing reasonably well academically, I knew deep down that the path of a tradesman was not meant for me. You know, sometimes in life, we have a clearer understanding of what we don't want rather than what we do want. I vividly recall the moment my parents asked me about my aspirations. I replied, "I think I need to go to university." However, when they pressed further and asked about my intended field of study, I found myself at a loss for words. The truth was, within my extended family, few of the males had pursued a university education. My father came from a family of thirteen children, while my mother came from a family of six children. The concept of attending university was relatively uncharted territory for male members of our family.

I was on the verge of becoming one of the first males in my extensive extended family to pursue a university education. To provide some context, I have a staggering sixty-four first cousins, most of whom are male. Given this context, my decision to attend university was rather unconventional. So, when I confessed that I had no idea what I was going to study, I genuinely meant it. My father, bless his soul, made a remarkable commitment. He took on a second part-time job on top of his full-time job to finance my education at the local boys' private school, paving the way for my journey to university. If it hadn't been for their unwavering support and financial sacrifices, I wouldn't be authoring this book.

Let me share another turning point in my life. I had been working in a corporate role for a university services division for a significant portion of my professional career. Alongside the leadership team, I had dedicated myself to building a substantial business within the organisation. However, a change in ownership brought forth a shift in the organisational philosophy. The decisions being made no longer aligned with the purpose I had initially embraced. It was at this juncture that I was presented with a redundancy package—a choice that was entirely optional. I still had the opportunity to retain my position if I so wished. Yet, I made the deliberate decision to accept the redundancy package, for it opened the door for me to embark on the journey of creating Organisations That Matter. Since then, I have never looked back, fully committed to this new path. Seventeen years later I continue to be blessed by that decision.

That specific turning point has had a profound impact on my life. It served as a catalyst for personal growth and self-discovery. I realised that the direction the organisation was compelled to take was not aligned with my own aspirations and values. I found myself at odds with the new path that had been set, despite having invested significant effort in establishing the organisation in the first place.

However, within that challenge, an opportunity revealed itself—a long-standing desire that had been quietly tugging at the corners of my mind. It was a pivotal moment where I had to confront the difficult reality of letting go while embracing the prospect of something new.

BACKGROUND RESEARCH

These three examples I've shared exemplify the power of turning points. I firmly believe that if any one of these pivotal moments hadn't occurred, or even if just one had been absent, I wouldn't be here with you now, guiding you through this program.

Please pause and use your notebook to complete the Turning Points exercise.

1. *Identify three to six turning points that if they had not occurred you would not be reading/ listening to this book at this moment in time.*

2. *Identify the significance of the turning point at the time it occurred. It may have been very significant, or not very significant. For example, when I was ten and my parents supported my going to a different school than my brothers, I didn't fully comprehend the significance of that support. After all, I was just a ten-year-old!*

3. *Identify the significance of the turning point now, as you look back. What are some key words that describe its significance?*

Well done! Many individuals find that when they reflect on their turning points, they discover a pattern of overcoming challenges and adversity. They recognise that despite the difficulties they encountered, things ultimately turned out for the better. In fact, some may even express gratitude for those trials, acknowledging that those experiences played a pivotal role in shaping their present contentment and fulfillment. Turning points possess an incredible power, serving as key insights into understanding one's Personal Purpose.

As you begin to uncover your turning points, new ones will emerge.

On September 2, 1988 I was involved in a head-on car accident. I was 19 and my girlfriend at the time was 18. We happened to be born on the same day, a year apart. We had just bought new stereo systems for our cars. My car was a red 1978 Toyota Corolla, and hers was a bright yellow 1980 Mazda 323 and we were super excited to have them installed over the weekend. It was a Friday night, just after 7 p.m., and we were driving back towards her house. It was raining. I was driving her car. Somehow, I missed noticing a car that was stopped ahead of us as it was turning right into a side street. In my effort to avoid that car, we slid into the oncoming traffic. I'll never forget my girlfriend throwing out her left arm and screaming, "Gary!!!" The next thing I knew I felt as if I had been crushed. She was unconscious and slouched towards me and I noticed some blood coming from her right ear. The car was a mess.

Three days earlier I had completed a Level Two First Aid course as part of my Physical Education Teaching Degree. I knew the blood was a bad sign and immediately attempted to get out of the car. As I tried to stand up, I fell, and a man caught me before I hit the ground. He lay me beside the car. It was chaos. As I lay there, I heard sirens. My head was spinning, but I believed I had to gather myself and help as soon as possible. I don't know if I lost consciousness, but it didn't seem very long before I got myself up from the ground. By this time police were already guiding traffic around the scene. As I came around to her side of the car, people were looking after her and holding her head. The car was completely crushed.

When the ambulance arrived, the paramedics went straight to her. Again, I don't know how long they spent with her. I wasn't assessed. I guess I was up and moving so they figured I must have been okay.

When they loaded her into the ambulance I asked if I could go with them, and they let me sit in the front seat.

Upon arrival at the hospital, they quickly took her away and sat me on a gurney in the hallway of the emergency department. It was chaos in the hospital that night. No one spoke with me for what seemed an eternity. I still had not been assessed.

Eventually a doctor came and asked me if I was the driver of the vehicle with the girl involved in the car accident. The first thing he said was that they believed she was going to die, and she needed to be transferred to St Vincent's Hospital immediately. A nurse then came and briefly assessed me and telephoned my family to notify them of the accident. This was before mobile phones, folks!

My brother Kelvin got to Box Hill Hospital in no time at all. My parents were away at the time.

My sole focus was to get out of Box Hill Hospital and get to St Vincent's Hospital, some 20 kilometres away. Somehow, I talked my way out of Box Hill Hospital (I still hadn't been properly assessed). I was in a lot of pain in my abdomen and agreed that if the pain persisted, I would check myself into the emergency department at St Vincent's Hospital.

Kelvin drove us to St Vincent's Hospital. When we arrived, her family were gathered around her, except her father who lived on the Sunshine Coast. As we walked in, they were understandably upset with me, and her grandfather expressed his anger towards me. I simply stood and wore it. What could I say! I had been the one driving the car, and it was her car I was driving. The accident was my fault. The reason she was lying on that hospital trolley was my fault.

She was quickly taken to intensive care where she was to be prepared for surgery. Her older sister and I stayed with her. Multiple times we were asked to leave the room because of her condition. She wasn't stable enough for surgery. Around 2 a.m. the following morning, her sister decided to go home. The nurses kept encouraging me to do the same, but I couldn't leave. Over the next three hours I was asked to leave the room several times due to all the alarms ringing. During this period, when I was sitting alone beside her, my mind was flooded by every time I had behaved as a possessive young man. You would think I would be remembering good times, but instead I was remembering how poorly I had behaved. I realised that it shouldn't be like that and that somehow, I had become completely focused on myself. I was selfish. I remember thinking, *How did this happen? How did I become this person? When I was 12, I was certain I would do something great with my life. But this! Here I am and I have ruined someone's life!* In that moment, I realised that I didn't have a clue about how to properly love someone. My parents had been wonderful examples of how to have a long-lasting, loving relationship, but somehow, I didn't have a clue. This was a shocking realisation to me: to metaphorically look yourself in the mirror and not be happy with who is staring back at you.

A little after 5 a.m., I was exhausted. She had stabilised to the point where the surgeons had decided to pause her brain surgery. If possible, it would be better if she could avoid it. Amazingly, other than a couple of minor cuts from the shattered glass, the only injury she had was the significant bleeding on her brain that had occurred from her brain smashing inside her skull. Her seatbelt had done its job.

I was in a lot of pain and a nurse persuaded me to go down to the emergency department and check myself in to hospital. For the first time since the accident, I was fully assessed and diagnosed with a bruised spleen. I was admitted to hospital.

Sometime on the Saturday afternoon, her father had arrived from the Sunshine Coast. He came to visit me, and my family let him have some time with me. He was surprisingly calm and simply asked me what had happened. He said he was glad I was okay and hoped I would recover soon. I am forever grateful for his compassion and empathy and have never forgotten it.

After three days I was released from the hospital. I immediately went to visit my girlfriend who had stabilised enough to be moved out of

BACKGROUND RESEARCH

intensive care and into a high care unit. Her family and I agreed we would take turns doing eight-hour shifts by her side, as she was still in a coma but was able to breathe on her own.

On the sixth day after the accident, her older sister and I were with her. It was mid-afternoon when a doctor entered her room and announced himself as the Head Neurosurgeon at the hospital. Up until that point, the nurses had been incredible with her, brushing her hair and keeping her neat and tidy, despite her lack of consciousness. The doctor walked up to the head of the bed, placed his hand on her forehead and shook her head from side to side. Her eyes popped wide open, and he poked her in one of her eyes. We were shocked. He then turned to us and told us that she would likely be in a vegetative state for the rest of her life and would never walk or talk. Her sister slapped him across the face and ran out crying. I was in disbelief. He then told me that the sooner we all understood what the rest of her life was going to be like, the better. A nurse came in and tidied her and brushed her hair. I was in shock. It had now been confirmed. I had completely ruined her life. That isn't a moment you ever forget.

I could feel emotion welling inside me, so I decided to go outside for some fresh air. As soon as I stepped onto the footpath at the bottom of the stairs, I broke down and started sobbing uncontrollably. It was the first time I had cried since the accident.

A trainee nurse who had completed a couple of shifts on my girlfriend's ward noticed me on her way into work. She stayed with me for forty-five minutes. She made herself late for work. I have never forgotten her kindness and unfortunately never saw her again to properly thank her for her generosity towards me.

Even to this day I can't fully describe how I felt at that time. The guilt from having ruined her life was immense.

Another four days later, while doing my shift at the hospital sitting beside her late on a Sunday afternoon, my great friend Mick, and another mate John, came to visit. Mick brought a teddy bear with him. A few minutes after he arrived, I felt as if I had been stabbed in the stomach. Bent over, I went to the bathroom. I was violently ill. Mick suggested I go back to emergency as maybe there was something very wrong with me. I had to make my way via the lift to the emergency department. When the lift doors opened, one of the doctors who had initially cared for me when I had been admitted was exiting the lift. Buckled over, I told her my symptoms. She recommended I get to emergency asap and walked away.

When in emergency I was assessed by an intern who diagnosed me with stomach cramps due to stress. Despite having access to my medical history, no tests were conducted. My family was contacted, and my brother-in-law John arrived forty-five minutes later to take me home. Due to my ongoing vomiting, I left the emergency department buckled over with a bucket in hand. We had to lay the seat flat in the car so I could put on my seatbelt and assume the foetal position on the way home.

I was assisted inside and went to bed. I didn't sleep at all due to the pain I was in. My mother called the local doctor around 11 a.m. the next day and he arrived at our home just before 3 p.m. I was extremely fit and lean at the time, and he said he couldn't tell if there was anything wrong with my spleen and believed that the best course of action was to follow the diagnosis from the hospital. As I hadn't slept, he gave me a sleeping pill, and I fell asleep. I awoke at 5:30 p.m. in incredible pain, and delirious. My dad had returned from work, and I vaguely remember him standing over me and saying something about being worried that I was dying. Truth be told, at that stage I was internally bleeding to death and had been bleeding for nearly twenty-four hours.

My mother called for an ambulance.

BACKGROUND RESEARCH

Three hours later, at approximately 8:30 p.m., the ambulance arrived. My father was beside himself. The ambulance officers were the first people to say that I had a ruptured spleen and would require emergency surgery. I was loaded into the ambulance and taken to the Monash Medical Centre where I underwent a splenectomy.

Sometime later I was informed the surgeons had removed nearly four litres of blood from my abdomen, which was an extensive job to ensure I didn't get any infections from the surgery. One nurse told me the surgeons had left me, "Clean as a whistle!"

Unfortunately, I experienced complications after my surgery, and I had a major blockage about 15 centimetres into my upper intestines. I'll save you all the gory details, but it took seventeen days before I was able to use my bowel and I lost 20 kg during that period. Finally, when my bowel started working, I was released from the hospital. I weighed 49 kg.

My twin brother's friend Nick collected me from the hospital and drove me directly to the rehabilitation hospital, some 42 kilometres across town, to visit my girlfriend who had been moved to that hospital a couple of weeks beforehand.

While she didn't know who I was due to her post-traumatic amnesia (and another reason we would discover sometime later) she spoke her first word that day.

Over the next eleven months, most days I drove to the hospital to spend time with her and to help with her rehabilitation. I was there when she fed herself for the first time, and when she took her first independent step. These were significant milestones.

We learned that the trauma she had suffered meant that she had lost about twenty months of her memory of the time preceding the accident. This meant our entire relationship was gone. This was extremely difficult to cope with because she would call me different names when I visited. It was a bit like the movie *50 First Dates*, if that makes sense.

There wasn't support back then like there is these days. You simply had to work out how to handle the situation by yourself. The fact is, I didn't handle it. I was a mess.

By March 1990 she had been home for nearly six months and was very eager to get married. She had made a dramatic recovery and while she continued to battle the effects of a brain injury, most people would not have immediately recognised what she had been through upon first meeting her. Our relationship was very different, and I felt a lot of pressure to marry her. Deep down, I knew that if I did marry her, it would be out of guilt, which wasn't the right reason to marry her.

I made the tough decision to end our relationship.

For the sake of the story, you should know she has led a full life and if you ever met her, you wouldn't know what she went through all those years ago. Her brain scans at the time fooled everyone. Years later as we all learned about brain plasticity, her story highlights how amazing the brain can be at creating new neural pathways. And to the Head Neurosurgeon from St Vincent's Hospital back on that day in 1988, you were wrong, buddy!

A fascinating part of this story is that my wife, Michelle, was late for work as an aerobics instructor due to the accident blocking the traffic on the way to take her class. Michelle literally drove her car around the accident! Michelle and I met later in November 1990 but didn't start dating until May 1991. When we first met, Michelle didn't want to come within 40 metres of me! While our meeting may have been love at first sight for me, it wasn't for her. I had some work to do and thankfully, she eventually changed her mind! It was love at six months for her ☺!

BACKGROUND RESEARCH

Early in 1991 I decided to start reading again. Other than academic books, I hadn't read a book since my last year in high school. The book I chose to read was *Seven Habits of Highly Effective People* by Stephen Covey. That book, and his subsequent book, *First Things First*, got me back on the path to the person I am today.

Around the time Michelle and I started dating, my father was diagnosed with cancer. My university degree had been delayed due to the accident, so I was completing it part time. My close friends had graduated or were in their final year of the course. Michelle had completed her degrees and was seeking full-time employment. I was the only one of the eleven children at home and helped Mum care for Dad.

In 1992 he had major surgery to remove his stomach cancer and after he recovered, he had a little under six months where he was as healthy as he had ever been. In late 1992 his cancer returned and unfortunately had spread to his bones. My close friends were heading overseas to teach in the United Kingdom and Michelle had started her first full-time job. I still had one semester to complete for my degree. Despite that, there was a temptation to defer my studies and join my friends overseas. Michelle would not have been able to come, and Mum needed help nursing Dad. I decided to stay home and am forever grateful for making that decision.

When I was helping Mum nurse Dad, I discovered I was able to 'handle' that situation. I suspect that because of my experience with the car accident, I was somehow equipped to be able to deal with that demanding situation. Because of what I was learning from Stephen Covey, I decided to be proactive and make the most of the situation with Dad. We had many long conversations and, while he may have been dosed to his eyeballs with morphine, he gave me many hugs and told me that he loved me, many times. I can still feel his hugs and hear his voice in my ear as I write this.

Those memories are a gift he gave me to carry with me for the rest of my life. My parents did the best they could raising all eleven of us. I don't recall Dad hugging me or telling me he loved me when I was little. I don't hold that against him. He showed love for us by working so hard, as did Mum. Again, I am forever grateful for the gift of hugs I received while nursing him.

My siblings gave me the honour of writing, with their assistance, and delivering his eulogy at his funeral. It was an incredible honour. He was seventy years old when he passed.

Your turning points can function as a shining light on something extremely powerful, your personal purpose.

Personal Purpose

Your personal purposes, alongside your values, serve as guiding lights illuminating your daily actions. They act as your personal North Star, keeping you on the path of authenticity. It is common for individuals to feel uncertain about their personal purpose. Like values, personal purpose can often be captured in a concise statement. What's fascinating is that personal purpose statements are not necessarily unique in themselves. What truly sets them apart is how they are translated into action. Interestingly, you may discover a connection between your turning points and your personal purpose. If we reflect on the turning point stories I shared earlier, a recurring theme emerges—choice.

For me, 'choice' played a significant role in each of the turning points I have shared with you. Some choices were made by me, others were made for me. Additionally, staying committed to those choices was crucial. My parents' willingness to stay with their choice to keep Denis and I in separate classrooms was profound for me. My choice to end the relationship with my girlfriend after the car accident was huge. My choice to start reading again was massive. My choice to remain home and nurse Dad became a gift.

One of my heroes is Robert K. Greenleaf. He argued that failing to act in the moment where action is possible, but often unpopular, in the pursuit of creating a desired future, is an ethical failure of leadership. My parents, despite their limited education, did not fail this test. They passed with flying colours. I am certain that their steadfastness in this situation enabled me to develop the independence I have demonstrated ever since I was that five-year-old boy.

Over time, I've come to realise that my personal purpose—the time when I feel truly alive and aligned with the life I am meant to lead, if such a notion exists—is when I assist individuals, teams, organisations and people like yourself participating in this program, in recognising the profound choices available to you. That, in essence, is my personal purpose.

That statement, encapsulating my purpose of enabling people to recognise their available choices, may not appear particularly unique on the surface. However, I can assure you that the way I live that purpose is absolutely distinctive. I do it in my own way. To better understand what I mean, consider the purpose, or mission statements you come across in organisations, perhaps even your own. It's remarkable how similar mission or purpose statements can be among organisations in the same or similar industries. Yet, the way they bring those statements to life is entirely different and unique.

The same principle applies to individuals. Now, I invite you to take a moment and press 'pause' to draft a concise statement that reflects what you believe your personal purpose might be.

Good work! Remember, personal purpose evolves over time and undergoes multiple iterations. My own personal purpose has gone through about ten drafts, and while they weren't drastically different, they gradually refined and now truly resonate with who I am and my life's mission across all my roles. If you're still unsure or drawing a blank, it's perfectly all right to frame it as a question: "I aspire to discover my purpose." This question can become part of your plan, and in one of the future chapters, we will explore the power of questions—how they can provide direction and focus, and ultimately help you create the success you desire. You don't have to possess all the answers right away.

I want to emphasise once again that you don't need to have all the answers. Your personal plan for success can involve a multitude of questions that provide you with focus and direction. It's about seeking out the answers to those questions. In a future chapter, we will delve deeper into this topic.

So, if you haven't yet completed that activity, take a moment to press 'pause' and finish it now. Remember, nothing worthwhile happens without constructive action. Choosing to progress without attempting the activity is also an action but highlights that not all action is equal. Many actions take you away from success. If you are going to act, and use the same amount of energy taking yourself away from success, why wouldn't you use that energy and act towards success?

You have now drafted your personal purpose or at the very least recognised the need to explore and discover what it might be. I encourage you to continue reflecting on your turning points as they can provide valuable insights into your personal purpose.

Congratulations! We have successfully navigated through Chapter 2. What's next? Chapter 3 awaits, where we will introduce you to the core concept that forms the foundation of the Yes For Success OTM Plan for Personal Success® program. I'm excited for you as you progress to this next step in the program!

CHAPTER 3

CORE CONCEPT

"Tension is the great integrity."

R. *Buckminster Fuller*

This concept is incredibly powerful, and its comprehension is vital as we embark on creating your Yes For Success OTM Plan for Personal Success®.

The core concept we are about to explore is known as 'creative tension'. My introduction to this concept came from a book called *The Fifth Discipline*, authored by Peter Senge in the early 1990s. Peter Senge, an esteemed academic and leadership expert affiliated with the Massachusetts Institute of Technology, specialises in the field of organisational learning. It is worth noting that one of Senge's mentors is a remarkable individual named Robert Fritz. Robert, renowned as both an artist and a film director, penned a book titled *The Path of Least Resistance*, in which he eloquently explains the concept of 'creative tension'.

The fascinating aspect of Peter and Robert's association lies in Robert's artistic background and his accomplishments in the film and music industries. Should you research Robert Fritz, you will discover valuable insights into the concept of creative tension. While my initial understanding of this concept came from Peter Senge, further exploration led me to recognise the immense power inherent in Robert Fritz's perspective. In fact, you might even consider pausing here to grab an elastic band, as it can provide a tangible demonstration of how this concept operates.

Assuming you have your elastic band ready, take one end and secure it around your pointer finger on your right hand, while the other end wraps around your pointer finger on your left hand. Separate your hands to ensure there is a noticeable distance between the two ends of the elastic band as you stretch the band. Observe the tension present in the elastic band as it stretches between your fingers. Picture your right hand, the upper one, representing your desired future—the future you aspire to achieve. On the other hand, your left hand symbolises your current reality, your present circumstances or starting point. While there exists a disparity between these two points, that tension holds within it stored energy, eager to bridge the gap and bring your present reality closer to your vision. Technically, this is called Potential Energy. The beauty of Potential Energy is that it wants to become Kinetic Energy—energy for action!

Let us bring your action to life. Take a moment to slowly bring your bottom hand, your left hand, towards your top hand, your right hand, and pay attention to how the tension and energy in the elastic band change during this process. You will observe that the energy and tension decrease as your bottom hand draws nearer to your top hand. As the gap reduces, so does the potential energy that you can turn into kinetic energy and use for action. This is why it is crucial to maintain a gap between your vision and your current reality. This gap serves as the wellspring of energy that propels you to act.

CORE CONCEPT

Let's explore what happens when there is no gap between your hands. Bring your hands together and observe what occurs with the energy in your elastic band. It vanishes. There is no longer any energy present. Perhaps you have experienced this in your life, or you may know individuals who feel utterly stuck, lacking the motivation to get out of bed in the morning, exercise, change their eating habits or mend relationships they themselves damaged. They lose the energy needed to act and shape the life they truly desire. It is important to note that the use of the word 'create' here is intentional.

By understanding the immense power of this core concept, we can actively 'create' the future we desire. We achieve this by ensuring there is always a gap between our vision and our present reality. This simple structure provides us with the energy necessary to take action and do what is required to bring our vision to life. However, as your present reality draws closer to your vision, it becomes crucial to re-envision. This is why I recommend implementing ninety-day plans as a minimum. If you have not already incorporated them into your routine, I strongly encourage you to do so. As you develop your plan, remember to review the entire strategy every six to twelve months. This allows you to reset your vision and ensure that this framework continues to work effectively for you. I'll cover this in more detail in Chapters 9 and 10.

While you focus on your vision, it is essential to recognise and celebrate your progress. Literally every day, notice, celebrate and be grateful for your progress. You will learn how powerful this is in later chapters. For now, start noticing the progress in anything you are doing on a personal or professional level. Stop, reflect, notice your progress, celebrate it and be consciously grateful. This simple habit is profoundly powerful in enabling you to live a harmonious life, which is why the concept and practice of creative tension is central to this book.

If you have previously attempted this kind of work in life and found that after a while, you weren't taking the necessary actions and stopped using this structure, it shouldn't come as a surprise if you ceased to create success.

Procrastination is a sign of creative tension being absent. You can use this core concept to overcome procrastination. When you are clear about the future and outcomes you wish to create, you become aware of what you will be sacrificing if you do not do whatever it is that you need to do to create it. When you have this level of clarity, it makes it easier to overcome procrastination because you know what you need to do, and what you will lose if you do not act.

Does this mean creative tension guarantees success? No, it doesn't. It does guarantee that success has a chance to be created. This is vital for you to understand. If you do not take action to create the outcomes you desire, you are guaranteed NOT to be successful. This is a fact.

If I did not write the words for this book, it would not matter how much I imagined the book being published, it would never happen. The book would have no chance of becoming a success. Only through deliberate action, authoring the book, recording the audio version, arranging for the cover to be designed and much more, does the book have a chance to be created and be successful. And along the way, I deliberately notice and am grateful for my progress which provides a degree of happiness and peace, today. I don't have to wait for the book to be completed to experience the happiness. Sure, there will be a major dose of happiness and peace when the book is completed, but most of our lives consist of the smaller versions of happiness. The problem is, we stop noticing them.

Right now, reflect on a goal. Use your notebook to identify the progress you made today, the past week or month. Be grateful. Literally write why you are grateful for your progress. Use that gratitude to give you the impetus to keep going.

By the end of this process of crafting your Yes For Success OTM Plan for Personal Success®, you will have a crystal-clear understanding of what you stand to miss out on if you don't follow through and bring your vision to life. Therefore, it requires discipline to maintain the essential gap between your vision and your current reality.

There is an additional benefit to embracing this concept, particularly when you develop your plan. Formal leaders, such as managers, business owners and bosses, must continually use creative tension to create success for their organisation, business units and teams. It is one of the reasons why they are leaders. They can see the gap between what is possible and what is presently unfolding. One of the challenges for leaders is effectively communicating the vision and inspiring others to join them on the journey of creating the future. However, this tension can also pose challenges for leaders due to the discrepancy between their present reality and the desired future.

Sometimes, the desired future is framed as moving away from the undesirable aspects of the present reality. You may have a job that you strongly dislike. All you can think about is working somewhere else. Leaving this job is your main driver. While that can be powerful, it is crucial to have positive elements in your future that you actively strive towards. Merely focusing on moving away from unwanted aspects of the present reality is insufficient. At the beginning, you may indeed have things in your current situation that you wish to move away from, but it is equally important, if possible, to recognise the positive aspects of what you want and actively include them in your envisioned future. Describe the type of work culture in which you would like to be employed. Imagine the quality of relationships you would like to have with your manager and colleagues. When you have this level of clarity in addition to the aspects of your current reality that you desire to move away from, the actions you take to create your future are more focused and specific to creating the full picture of what you want.

Imagine being in a situation where you find yourself trapped in a bad relationship. Naturally, your inclination is to move away from that negative dynamic. However, when you envision your future, you see yourself in a strong, healthy relationship, where each of you are helping each other grow individually and as a couple. It is the type of relationship that you imagine, rather than focusing on a specific person. Who the person is could be the same person as your current partner, or someone new. Your focus, what you want for your future, is the strong relationship and everything that comes with that type of relationship. When imagining this future, you focus on what you want from a healthy relationship perspective.

The concept of the elastic band, which represents creative tension, is extraordinarily powerful. It permeates the entire planning process, as you will discover. At this point, I want to acknowledge Jock MacNeish for providing the accompanying illustrations.

I invite you to pause and take a moment to reflect on the first illustration. If you're engaging in this exercise with a partner, I encourage you to have a conversation about what insights and revelations this illustration sparks in relation to your understanding of success.

If you are listening to the audiobook version, please visit www.orgsthatmatter.com/yfsresources to view the illustrations.

CORE CONCEPT

Figure 5 Steps For Success by Jock MacNeish

When reviewing this illustration during my in-person workshops, many participants have shared their insights on the process of creating success. They have emphasised that it is a step-by-step journey with specific actions to take. However, some people have raised valid points about the order of these steps and how they might vary based on individual circumstances. For instance, someone might already have a good financial situation but lack self-awareness and education. In such cases, the traditional sequence of steps may not be applicable. Additionally, others have expressed that they view these steps as interconnected and ongoing, requiring consistent attention.

And do you know what? They are absolutely right. Moving from our present reality to our desired future, whether it is in our career, health, relationships, finances, education or self-awareness, requires us to work on multiple aspects simultaneously. It is an integrated approach.

YES FOR SUCCESS

That is why I commissioned Jock to create this second illustration. Take a moment now to pause and deeply contemplate this illustration. Reflect on what it communicates to you and the insights it triggers.

Figure 6 Balance Wheel For Success by Jock MacNeish

Many people have noticed the person depicted in the background of the illustration. Which elements of their wheel are missing? We deliberately left the details unreadable. Why? Because it symbolises the fact that regardless of which three out of the six elements they have mastered, there are still missing pieces. From a societal perspective, someone may be deemed successful if they have achieved financial stability and career progress. However, true success encompasses a broader spectrum of areas that collectively contribute to a fulfilling and balanced life.

CORE CONCEPT

But here's the truth: Even if someone has wealth and career status, they can still find themselves stuck if they're missing out on other crucial elements such as relationships, health, a well-rounded education or a mindset of lifelong learning. I've had the opportunity to work with individuals in such situations. They come to me because they feel trapped, realising that they aren't truly happy and aren't achieving the success they desire. Now, let's take a closer look at the person depicted on this wheel. I often pose a question to the audiences I engage with: Does it seem like an easy balancing act? Most people respond with, "Probably not."

And they're right. It's not easy; creating success requires effort and commitment. However, by embracing this balancing act, we gain focus, clarity and a deep understanding of what we stand to miss out on if we neglect certain areas. So, why not give it a try? Although it may be challenging, it's a worthwhile endeavour.

Now, let me ask you another question: Who do you think is happier between these two individuals portrayed in the illustration? It's fascinating that 99% of people I've asked have identified the person at the top of the wheel as the happier one. This reinforces the notion that while it may be demanding to maintain balance, those who strive for equilibrium are more likely to experience greater happiness than those who only focus on specific parts of their wheel.

And this is absolutely spot-on. I want to emphasise that I'm not suggesting that happiness should be postponed until the future, that we should endure hardship now with the hope that happiness will come later. After all, life is unpredictable, and anything can happen at any moment. You could literally get hit by a bus tomorrow!

That's why it's crucial to cultivate as much happiness as possible in your present life. By doing so, you increase the likelihood of experiencing an equal or even greater level of happiness in the future. Trust me, when you're actively engaged in the balancing act on this wheel, you become more attuned to moments of happiness. It could be completing a 10-kilometre run, rejoining an indoor soccer team, addressing a health issue by seeking medical attention, or achieving success in your career or a specific project. How do you feel when you accomplish these things?

It brings you joy and contentment. You might also notice moments of personal growth and self-awareness. For instance, you might catch yourself resisting the urge to react negatively towards someone, a behaviour that used to be your default. Recognising the destructiveness of such behaviour, you consciously restrain yourself, and as you walk out of a meeting, you think to yourself, *I'm genuinely proud of myself. I showed emotional intelligence and self-control.*

These moments of success and personal development elicit a sense of happiness and pride. So, let's not underestimate the importance of finding happiness in the present while working towards a brighter future. It's about embracing the journey and celebrating the milestones along the way. It is about being tuned in to the happiness that is available in your life, right now.

It could manifest in various aspects of your life. It might be a breakthrough in your relationships, or perhaps you successfully save some money. Speaking of relationships, imagine when one of your children does something that you've been diligently teaching them, the moment they stand up for what's right or make a wise choice. It fills your heart with joy. I experienced this firsthand when my fifteen-year-old son, Aiden, and my twelve-year-old son, Darcy, decided to help me write this book while on school holidays. With all the other choices available to them, they chose to help me. I can't express how happy and proud I felt in that moment. Similarly, my eighteen-year-old son, Callum, has been learning social media marketing while on a break from his performing arts study. Seeing his enthusiasm for learning a

CORE CONCEPT

new skill and the great outcomes he has been achieving creates joy for me. That's pure happiness. This is happening right here, right now, while we are doing the work to create more success and happiness in the future. Being present and supporting my youngest son when his team won their junior football Grand Final was pure joy, especially given the small role I had accepted to play in helping the team be successful.

Working through the balance on this wheel can bring immense joy. However, I must emphasise that in reality, the different parts or 'key elements' of the wheel aren't necessarily equal. We've depicted them equally for the sake of the diagram, but in practice, certain elements will take precedence at different times. For instance, when starting a new job, your career may demand a significant portion of your attention. Similarly, pursuing postgraduate or undergraduate education or entering a profession like the police force will require a major investment of time and energy in education. Each key element will have its own season of prominence.

The critical point here, and where many people often stumble in their pursuit of success, is understanding that while certain areas may demand intense focus, it's essential to maintain balance and attend to the other aspects as well. So, even if you're fully engrossed in your studies or career, don't neglect your health and fitness. Don't allow those areas to fade into the background; otherwise, you risk becoming the person depicted at the back of the illustration—a person missing essential elements of a fulfilling life. You may have a meditation technique that works for you. Find a way to maintain that technique when you are extremely busy in another area of your life. For example, I have a range of meditations I listen to, and some are as long as thirty minutes, and some are as short as five minutes. I defer to the five-minute versions when required, but I maintain the practice because I know how valuable it is.

It is crucial for you to grasp the significance of finding balance among these six key elements, and that's precisely what your plan aims to achieve. As you progress through the chapters, you will incorporate the necessary details to enable you to be specific about what you need for your circumstances. Remember, it is essential not to overlook any of these elements. You must allocate time and effort to maintain each one. Even if you have multiple tasks and commitments in your career or education, make sure you have at least one action item in health, relationships, wealth for life, and other key areas. Consider this as a seed I'm planting now. Moving forward, it is vital that you actively engage in each of these key areas to shape the future you desire.

As you can see, the arrow points to the 'future' sign, indicating the need to consistently readjust your elastic band. In the upcoming chapters, you will delve into defining the timeframe for your plan. However, for now, what timeframe will you set at the top of your elastic band? Keep in mind that timeframes can be flexible, as we all have different preferences. Some may feel more comfortable with shorter-term plans, while others lean towards longer-term horizons. Statistically, more people tend to favour shorter-term goals. Nevertheless, it is important to challenge yourself regardless of the timeframe you choose. It could encompass your entire life, including retirement, or perhaps focus on key age milestones, such as five to ten years or one to five years. If you have significant events on the horizon, I strongly recommend considering the event itself along with an additional year beyond its occurrence.

Let's explore the concept of stretching your timeframe a bit further. If your initial goal is set for when you turn thirty, consider aiming for thirty-one instead. It's remarkable how much of a difference this 'plus one' effect can make in the power of your plan. By thinking just slightly beyond your immediate target, you introduce a level of tension that can be highly impactful. I understand that it may be challenging,

CORE CONCEPT

but ideally, you don't want the top part of your elastic band to be too easy or comfortable, it needs to contain some degree of tension.

It's crucial that you focus on a timeframe that feels somewhat uncomfortable, Then, commit to it.

The Power of Big Questions

When envisioning your desired future, you can include statements like: "I will have found the answers to some of my burning questions, such as ..." This is particularly powerful when considering your life as a whole. At the top of your elastic band, your vision can encompass having discovered the answers to various questions. Currently, you don't have to know what those answers are. This is often a stumbling block for many individuals when it comes to creating personal success plans; they feel uncertain about their answers.

However, there is one answer you do know: you want to uncover the answers to your current questions in your future. You aim to have discovered the solutions that resonate with you personally. So, what might some of those big questions be? Take a moment to reflect on them.

Please have your notebook ready. You will complete a two-step process to identify clarity and focus from your Big Questions. Let's move on to Step One. We'll be working through this process together, and I'll provide you with some examples along the way. In Step One, your task is to identify the questions that you would like to have answered in your desired future.

Allow me to share a couple of examples of what these questions might look like. One question could be: "What are the characteristics of work that I will find fulfilling?" Currently, at the top of your elastic band, you don't have the answer to this type of question.

Another example could be: "What types of physical activities will I enjoy doing on a regular basis?"

Moving on to Step Two. Once you've written down your questions in Step One, you want to transform these questions into outcome statements.

Let's use our previous questions as examples. The first question, "What are the characteristics of work that I will find fulfilling?" can be transformed into an outcome statement such as: "I will know the characteristics of the work that I will find fulfilling." This becomes your answer at the top of your elastic band—your desired future. On the other hand, the bottom of your elastic band represents the present reality: "Currently, I don't know the characteristics of the work that I will find fulfilling." You can see how we establish the structure of the elastic band, separating your desired outcome and your current situation for each of these questions.

Let's consider example two. You would change the question "What types of physical activities will I enjoy doing on a regular basis?" to "I will know what type of types of physical activity I will enjoy doing on a regular basis." In this way you have transformed your questions into outcome statements, recognising that in your present reality, at the bottom of your elastic band, you currently lack the answers to those questions.

Humans are exceptional explorers. Our ability to explore has shaped the world we inhabit. As you embark on the journey to uncover the answers to your questions, your inherent exploratory spirit will come to the forefront.

CORE CONCEPT

You are about to embark on a quest of self-discovery, where the answers you seek will be revealed. This is precisely what your plan entails. So, when you find yourself exploring and encounter a dead end, is it a negative outcome? Absolutely not. Simply mark a cross through that dead end and say, "No, this path doesn't lead me where I want to go. I will now venture down a new path." Contrast this with the belief that there is only one correct answer. If you reach a dead end, it can feel catastrophic, as if the sky is falling.

Understanding the power of exploration is transformative. To achieve the success you desire, you must embrace the idea of exploration. Undoubtedly, there will be aspects of your future where you currently lack the answers to your questions. However, you possess the questions themselves, and that is where their beauty lies. As we explored in Chapter 1, at the Level One Chart, questions provide us with remarkable focus and clarity, particularly at the top level, which represents the longer-term, whole-of-life perspective. As we progress through the charts, moving the Level Two Charts to Level Three Charts, the timeframes for your steps become progressively shorter and more immediate.

The Level Two Charts and Level Three Charts are fractals of the Level One Chart. If you're unfamiliar with fractals, they are structures that repeat the same pattern within themselves, much like a snowflake or a sprouting broccoli. It's a recurring pattern that echoes throughout. You may have experienced a similar phenomenon while standing in a lift with mirrors on opposite sides, observing multiple reflections of yourself stretching into the distance. This same concept applies to your planning for personal success with the elastic bands—it becomes fractalized, replicated from your Level One Chart down to your Level Three Charts.

Consider your Level One Chart, where we can draw inspiration from the artist Robert Fritz. Imagine your future as a blank canvas, waiting to be filled. At the outset, you have a rough idea, an outline of what you want to create. As you progress through the process of building your plan, particularly when we reach the Level Two Charts, you'll notice an interesting phenomenon. The impact of this iterative process begins to influence your Level One Chart, enhancing your clarity regarding your envisioned future. By delving into greater detail, exploring, and uncovering the answers to your questions, you gain a deeper understanding of the picture you are creating.

It's like refining the artwork on the canvas, adding layers of depth and nuance as you go. Each level of detail you explore has a ripple effect, illuminating your path and contributing to a clearer vision of the future you desire.

Once you have the answers to your questions, your focus and clarity expand, even at the whole-of-life level. It's a continuous journey of iteration and refinement. Your initial plan won't be as robust as your tenth plan. It's natural for strategies and actions to evolve and improve over time. That's why you can use this book or the *Yes For Success* Online Course to continue to review and update your plan over time.

Your plans will become more refined, your actions more effective, and your ability to shape the future you desire will sharpen. As you create more and more of the success you desire, your confidence grows and you know that you are using a system that works, breeding more confidence.

Master This System!

If you approach your plan as a one-time endeavour, you may experience some level of success, but it won't reach its full potential. As an adult, you often expect to excel at something the first time you try it, but the reality is that your initial attempts may only be a 3, 4, 5, 6 or 7 out of 10. I wrote about this concept and called it The Learning Curve in my Amazon Kindle #1 Bestseller *Disruption Leadership Matters:*

CORE CONCEPT

lessons for leaders from the pandemic. The message here is that it's crucial to acknowledge that there is always room for improvement in the planning process.

This iterative cycle allows you to grow and excel. The clarity of the whole-of-life vision becomes increasingly vivid as you navigate the process of building and creating. Returning to the idea of an artist filling in a canvas, the image they seek to create becomes clearer with each stroke. Initially, it's just an outline, slightly fuzzy, but as they progress, the image sharpens. Similarly, as you construct your plan, your vision will become clearer and more defined. It's perfectly acceptable to adapt and adjust as newfound clarity emerges during our journey.

I'd like to share some insights on the concept of visioning from someone who taught me valuable lessons, Dewitt Jones. Dewitt, a renowned *National Geographic* photographer, found a striking resemblance between his work in photography and the idea of personal visioning. Let's explore some of the lessons Dewitt learned through his passion for vision, which I believe are worth sharing with you.

One of Dewitt's key teachings is the importance of keeping our vision focused. I'll delve deeper into this topic in a later chapter, and you'll see how the chapters complement and build upon each other. By physically keeping your vision in front of your eyes, you create a constant reminder of the future you desire to create. Vision boards, consisting of photos or images that reflect your desired future, can be a powerful tool. If you are a visually oriented person, you may find it beneficial to gather pictures and display them in your home or office, serving as reminders of what you're striving to achieve. According to scientists from Rochester University's Centre for Visual Science, 50% of our neocortex is dedicated to vision; it is reasonable to argue that we are all visually oriented. A vision board has a high probability of being useful for everyone.

When constructing your plans, it's crucial to embrace a slower pace. Allow yourself the time and space to let clarity emerge. This is why I encourage you to progress through the chapters step by step, without skipping any. Each chapter has been thoughtfully structured to guide you on your journey, facilitating the emergence of clarity and insight.

Allow yourself to slow down and be patient as the chapters flow seamlessly into one another. It is in this state of patience and openness that your answers and clarity will emerge. Take a moment to stop, look and listen as we construct your Yes For Success OTM Plan for Personal Success®. Throughout this process, you'll generate numerous ideas, but it's through focused attention that you can discern what truly matters. Some things may seem nice to have, but they aren't the most important. It's essential to let them fall away.

Focus on identifying the best aspects of the future you desire and be willing to let go of the rest. Trust your intuition in this journey. Robert K Cooper, in his book *The Other 90%*, introduces the idea that our brain resides not only within our heads but also in two other significant areas of our bodies: around our heart and within our gut. Neuroscientific research supports this notion, showing the interconnectedness of these regions via our spinal cord. Cooper poses the question: Do we possess three brains or one brain existing in three parts of our body?

Our heart-brain represents our connection to others, while our gut-brain embodies our intuition, the innate knowledge of what is right or wrong. The head-brain represents our logical thinking. According to Cooper, it is crucial to engage all three brains. While we may have preferences for one or two of them, we must harness the power of all three. Dewitt Jones echoes this sentiment, emphasising the importance of trusting our intuition. It is through our intuition that we gain insights into the future we desire. Vishen Lakhiani, founder of Mindvalley.com and author of *The Code of the Extraordinary Mind*, passionately argues that intuition is essential for a successful life.

CORE CONCEPT

Your future and intuition are intimately connected, so it's crucial to listen to your intuition as you construct your plan. Dewitt Jones also suggests that it's not trespassing to venture beyond your self-imposed boundaries. In Chapter 2, we discussed the power of mental models. This serves as a gentle reminder from Dewitt and me that your mental models need to be challenged. You must be willing to question your mental models about success, ensuring that your own boundaries don't hinder your pursuit of the success you desire. Vishen Lakhiani advocates that everything in our lives starts with our mindset. Through changing your mental models, you can influence reality. I believe this to be true, because I have lived this myself, many times over. While I wasn't a 'complete' selfish person when I was nineteen and involved in the car accident, it is true that too many of the characteristics of a self-centred person were present in my life at that time.

The disruption to my life that the accident created was an opportunity to reassess how I saw the world. I did not know about mental models at that time, which is one of the reasons why I am so passionate about teaching them to everyone, young and old. When I learned about the concept some seven years later, I immediately recognised them and understood that I had decided to change them, especially when I decided to start reading again.

Your vision must be expansive, and not overly specific at the Level One Chart, to create countless opportunities for its realisation. Let's consider an example of having a vision that is too narrow. If I were to say, "I want to be the CEO of Disney", it would be too narrow.

While it's a commendable vision, it would be overly restrictive. The key question to ask is, "Why do I want to be the CEO of Disney?" Perhaps the answer is: *I aspire to lead a renowned organisation with a global brand that brings happiness, like Disney. I desire to work for a global organisation with a vast workforce. I yearn to be part of an organisation that impacts thousands upon thousands of lives.*

Imagine being part of an organisation in the entertainment industry, spreading happiness to countless individuals. If you've listed all those characteristics, it's important to recognise that Disney isn't the sole institution where you could offer your talents. The reality is that only one person can be the CEO of Disney at any given time. This doesn't mean you can't become the CEO of Disney, but it does mean that there are numerous alternative opportunities to bring your vision to life.

To illustrate further, when I was a young boy, I dreamt of playing elite football in Australia. Unfortunately, I wasn't naturally gifted with exceptional skills (my twin brother Denis seemed to have all of that!). Nonetheless, I excelled at the suburban level and displayed unwavering persistence. Although I didn't reach the top level as a player, as an adult and a professional, I had the opportunity to work in elite sport in Australia. I stood in the field in front of more than eighty-four thousand supporters at the Melbourne Cricket Ground, alongside players and coaches, engaging in leadership work at that level. I sat in the coaches' box and on the interchange bench. I was paid for my leadership skills and was involved in the highest level of Australian Rules Football in the country. I found a different way to contribute and bring my vision of being part of elite sport in Australia to life. While I didn't get to kick a football or become a star on the field, I was able to make a meaningful impact through various endeavours over time. I spent seven seasons involved in the highest level of Australian Rules Football. Not bad for a kid who couldn't kick a ball properly!

Therefore, ensure that your vision is vast enough to encompass a multitude of possibilities for making it a reality. Embrace the idea that there are countless paths to creating the future you desire. I suggest you should aim to have a Level One Chart vision that is vast enough to allow one thousand opportunities to bring it to life.

CORE CONCEPT

Dewitt's final suggestion is an intriguing one: "Do you have juice in your camera?" This seamlessly leads us to our next topic: Chapter 4: Passion.

Passion can be likened to the juice in your camera, as Dewitt recounts a story of a young boy who accompanied him while taking photographs. The boy had a makeshift camera, which happened to resemble a juice bottle. As Dewitt engaged in his photography, the boy finally looked up and took a sip of his juice, asking, "Does your camera have juice in it?" Dewitt, realising the metaphor the child was hinting at, responded, "No, I don't have juice in my camera." "Mine does!" exclaimed the boy!

What a lesson! Does your camera have juice in it? Do you have passion? This is what you will explore next in Chapter 4: Passion.

CHAPTER 4

PASSION

"Passion is energy. Feel the power that comes from focusing on what excites you."
Oprah Winfrey

The essence of creating a personal success plan revolves around the idea that when we express our passions, we ignite a profound energy within our lives. Reflect upon those moments in your life when you had the opportunity to embrace your passions. How alive did you feel? One of my passions is riding my motorbike. It's not merely a means of commuting; I indulge in it for recreational purposes. I organise two separate four-day tours each year with some of my closest friends who share this passion. Every moment spent on that bike invigorates my senses. Part of it stems from the inherent risks involved in this thrilling pursuit, where my life hangs by a thread, reliant on my skills and caution. Yet, I find myself truly alive and utterly present during those exhilarating rides. It's as if I merge with the machine, experiencing a sense of pure magic.

There is an undeniable sense of vitality and elation that engulfs individuals when they engage in activities that resonate with their passions. Whether it be singing, playing sports, conducting research or immersing oneself in meaningful work, these pursuits have the power to ignite a profound fire within. Personally, I consider myself incredibly fortunate because when I deliver the content in this program to live audiences, or when working with a coaching client on their plan, I experience an overwhelming sense of aliveness and rejuvenation. The very nature of the subject matter I discuss fuels my energy, reminding me of the immense significance of having passion present in our lives. This energy helps me to fully commit to my role as a facilitator, because I know the energy will flow from me to the audience, and back again.

Why is passion so vital? It serves as an indispensable wellspring of energy as you strive to create the success you yearn for. Let's face it, on the path to achieving your goals, there will be occasions when you must undertake tasks that may not ignite your enthusiasm. During such phases, it is your passion that becomes the driving force, sustaining you through the challenges and propelling you forward. It is this passion that acts as a catalyst for personal success.

Some of you may feel that you have never truly experienced passion in your life. Perhaps you struggle to recall a time when it was an integral part of your existence or believe it was something you embraced in your younger years. I emphatically argue that passion is an essential ingredient for a fulfilling life. So, if you have a penchant for singing or playing a musical instrument, ask yourself, when was the last time you wholeheartedly immersed yourself in that pursuit? When did you last feel the fire of passion coursing through your veins?

Let me clarify that when I speak of passion, I am not suggesting that it must be a constant presence in your everyday life, nor does it necessarily have to be associated with monetary compensation. While it's fantastic if your passion aligns with your profession, what truly matters is having passion present in some aspect of your life, where you know it will make an appearance. Take, for instance, those individuals whose passion lies in travelling. Although they may not have the luxury of travelling all the time due to work commitments and the need to earn a living, they ensure that their next travel experience is booked well in advance, providing them with something to look forward to, even if it's a year away. While waiting for the next trip to arrive, they research and explore what they will do on their trip, enabling them to 'experience' travel even when they aren't doing it. This stimulates passion and the subsequent benefits.

Even in such scenarios, where passion may not be a constant presence, it can still fill you with energy. That is precisely what we are discussing here. Drawing energy from your passion. Allow me to share a brief anecdote about one of my former clients, Cheryl.

Cheryl was in the process of crafting her individual plan for personal success. At the time, she held a significant position as a National Manager, focusing on safety within an organisation. During one of our conversations, she confided in me about her long-held passion. As a single mother in her early forties, Cheryl bravely expressed, "You know what, I've always harboured this intense desire to learn a musical instrument, yet I've never had the opportunity to pursue it."

In response, I suggested, "Well, let's include it in your personal success plan." Little did I anticipate the astonishing turn of events that would follow. When I reconnected with Cheryl in March of the subsequent year to check on her progress, she joyously shared that she had recently performed live on stage in front of an enthralled audience of over one hundred and fifty people. Remarkably, she skilfully played six songs on the saxophone, of all instruments!

It is truly wondrous how, after incorporating her musical passion into her personal success plan, the irresistible force of the law of attraction began to unfold. A kind-hearted friend gifted Cheryl a saxophone, and much to her surprise, she was able to coax delightful sounds from it. A feat that eludes most beginners in their initial attempts. Through the power of synchronicity, she was introduced to a talented saxophone instructor who guided her in honing her skills. Serendipitously, Cheryl discovered that a local hotel was hosting auditions for aspiring musicians to form bands. With unbridled enthusiasm, she raised her hand when they sought a saxophonist, and destiny smiled upon her as she stood as the only person with their hand raised, ready to embark on this extraordinary musical journey. As if it were 'meant to be', Cheryl was the only saxophonist at the audition.

Cheryl's story exemplifies the profound impact of aligning one's passion with a personal success plan. As she ventured forth on this transformative path, a harmonious convergence of events occurred, setting the stage for her triumphant musical debut. It serves as a testament to the unfathomable possibilities that emerge when we embrace our passions and allow the forces of the universe to guide us towards the fulfillment of our dreams.

Allow me to recount an extraordinary turn of events that unfolded in Cheryl's life. Despite juggling numerous responsibilities in her personal and professional spheres, Cheryl embarked on a transformative journey that began with a simple act—writing down her deepest desires. This powerful act of clarity illuminated her path, revealing an insatiable yearning she had carried within for years.

Driven by an unwavering determination, Cheryl took bold steps towards her dream. And lo and behold, one thing led to another, and she found herself standing on a stage, adorned in the vibrant aura of a band. For someone as busy as Cheryl, this achievement was a testament to the sheer power of commitment and the written word. The experience of being in the spotlight, of materialising a lifelong aspiration that had once seemed impossible, was an indescribable joy for her.

What's truly awe-inspiring is that this remarkable transformation unfolded at a pace that surpassed even Cheryl's wildest expectations. Merely seven months prior, she had believed that this dream would take a minimum of five years to realise. Yet, propelled by her focused pursuit of personal success, she defied all odds and accomplished her goal in record time.

I share Cheryl's remarkable story to ignite a spark within you, to prompt reflection upon your own passions and aspirations. Just as Cheryl discovered the astonishing power of clarity and intention, I implore you to pause and contemplate what truly ignites your soul. What pursuits bring you immense joy and fulfillment? By embracing your passions and directing your energy towards them, you, too, can unlock a world of endless possibilities.

As you embark on this transformative journey, remember Cheryl's triumphant tale and the extraordinary speed with which her dreams materialised. Allow her story to inspire and embolden you, for within the depths of your passion lies the key to unlocking your own personal success.

If you find yourself in a position where you have never experienced the exhilaration of passion in your life, fret not. For we, as humans, are endowed with an extraordinary spirit of exploration. You can embrace this aspect by incorporating a specific goal into your plan— an aspiration to uncover a passion previously unknown to you. As we delved into in Chapter 3, you can transform this desire into an outcome statement, such as: *"I will discover my passions and wholeheartedly engage with them in my daily life."* This statement shall take its place in your Level One Chart, nestled within the vision section. And so, to embark on this quest, you must adopt the mental model of an intrepid explorer.

With the mindset of an explorer, imagine a scenario where a friend unexpectedly invites you to join them in an evening of Latin dancing on a Thursday night. Should you find yourself free, and in the spirit of exploring your passions, you might seize the opportunity and respond with a resounding "Yes!" You would venture forth and give it a try.

PASSION

In doing so, you open the door to the possibility of a wondrous revelation. As you immerse yourself in the dance, a moment of epiphany might strike: *"Oh my, this is absolutely incredible! I adore it!"* And just like that, you have stumbled upon a newfound passion. Alternatively, your exploration may lead you to the realisation that while the experience was enjoyable, it simply did not resonate with you.

Embrace the spirit of exploration as you traverse the path to uncovering your passions. Say "yes" to the opportunities that arise, allowing yourself to venture into uncharted territory. Through this intrepid journey, you will unearth the passions that stir your soul, guiding you towards a life brimming with fulfillment and purpose.

Having determined that Latin dancing may not be your avenue of passion, you graciously acknowledge that there are countless other possibilities awaiting your exploration. Remaining open to new experiences is paramount in your quest to discover your true passion. It could be that your passion lies in supporting a team like the Western Bulldogs in the Australian Football League, an organisation and team that I, too, hold dear to my heart. I am fortunate to be able to attend matches and cheer on my beloved team. Passion has a way of entering our lives through various avenues.

The crux of the matter lies in the present moment; do you possess a passion that invigorates you? Can you incorporate this passion into your plan, allowing it to infuse you with the energy necessary to navigate life's arduous and challenging tasks?

If you have yet to do so, please take the time to consider your passions. Take a moment to take out your notebook and answer this pivotal question: What ignites your passion? It is entirely acceptable if your response is currently a blank canvas, devoid of any specific passion. You may even find yourself writing "nothing" at this moment. However, I implore you to delve deeper and contemplate: What are the aspects of life that stir your soul, even if they are not currently in existence? Maybe you played the piano when you were a child, and you loved playing it. Then, other things got in the way as you got older, and you stopped playing. Yet, when you reflect on playing the piano when you were younger, a smile breaks across your face. Your smile may hint that playing the piano was once a passion. Consider playing the piano again as part of your exploration. Embrace this opportunity to explore and identify the passions that lie dormant within you. By doing so, you shall infuse your life with purpose, vitality and unwavering enthusiasm.

Have you ever noticed those moments when time seems to evaporate? It's as if the hands of the clock cease their perpetual motion. Such instances often occur when we are engrossed in certain types of work, completely losing track of time. It could be the captivating pages of a novel that transport us to another world, the profound narratives within autobiographies or perhaps a specific field of study that ignites your passion, causing time to slip away unnoticed.

Take a moment to reflect on your own life. How is your passion currently intertwined with your existence? Does it manifest itself in any way, shape or form?

Consider your career — does it align with your passion in any capacity? Does your current path allow your passion to flourish, or do you envision a future where your career and passion harmoniously intertwine?

These questions prompt you to delve deeper into the nature of your aspirations. They encourage you to evaluate the role passion plays in your daily life and how you can leverage it to shape your future endeavours. Ponder these queries earnestly, for they hold the potential to illuminate the path towards a life infused with purpose and satisfaction.

Many individuals embark on career changes to ensure their passion remains at the forefront of their lives. They find a way to make it possible, carving a new path that aligns with their deepest aspirations.

Have you ever experienced a shift in your passions as time unfolds? I certainly have. And you know what? That's perfectly all right. In fact, I consider myself incredibly fortunate to have kept passion alive and burning within me throughout my journey.

Part of discovering your passion involves understanding how your energy works. I have published an eBook entitled *Energy for Success – Seven steps for Generating the Energy You Need for Success*. Because you have purchased this book, you can get the eBook for free. Simply enter the Coupon **EneryForSuccess** (all one word) at the checkout and you will get the eBook for free!

While having a well-crafted plan is crucial, equally important is having the energy to put that plan into action. These two elements go hand in hand, driving you towards your desired outcomes.

After completing this chapter, I encourage you to delve into the enriching materials within the *Energy for Success* eBook.

Imagine riding a bicycle. Your *Yes For Success* plan is like the handlebars that you use to steer your way along your path. Pushing on the pedals propels you forward. Understanding how your energy works gives you the power to push on your pedals. Therefore, having a plan and an understanding how to generate the energy to propel you forward are both essential for creating the life you desire.

Now, let's touch upon a couple of additional factors worth delving into—your personality preferences. Researching this aspect can offer valuable self-awareness and contribute to your personal growth. Numerous tools are available for this purpose, such as Myers-Briggs, DISC, Wave, e-Colours, What Makes People Tick and more.

Understanding your personality preferences can unlock a deeper understanding of yourself and how you relate to others. It's a valuable tool on your path to personal and professional success.

It's essential to take a moment and document your personal strengths and weaknesses in your notebook. Creating personal success necessitates a high level of self-awareness regarding these aspects. Understanding your areas of proficiency and areas where you may need improvement is crucial. This understanding allows you to recognise and appreciate the skills and talents of others who excel in areas where you may not be as proficient.

Let me emphasise this point once again: For your personal success, it is vital to develop the ability to identify and appreciate the strengths of others that complement your own weaknesses. This requires a deep awareness of your own strengths and weaknesses. Additionally, it is equally important to recognise how your strengths can complement the weaknesses of others. This understanding will enable you to form high-performing teams and establish collaborative relationships that benefit everyone involved.

The happiest people I know are the ones who work in the intersection of their passions and talents. I am one of those people! When you know your passions and talents, it is amazing how big this intersection can be. If you aren't sure about the talents you possess, I urge you to visit Renata Bernarde's *The Job Hunting* podcast and use her talent identification tool Talentpredix – it is brilliant!

Now, let's move on to Chapter 5, which focuses on Personal Vision. This chapter presents an exciting opportunity for you to articulate and record what you desire in your personal vision.

PERSONAL VISION

"The only thing worse than being blind is having sight but no vision."

Helen Keller

Personal Vision is the phase where you articulate and document precisely what you envision for your desired future. It's an exhilarating segment of the program. By now, you have laid the groundwork through extensive background research, and the time has come for you to put pen to paper and provide answers for your personal vision.

To achieve this, you will follow a two-step process that will ultimately lead to the formulation of a Level One Chart vision. This refers to the overarching vision for your entire life, encompassing the longest possible timeframe, setting the stage for the rest of your plan. Firstly, I will present a series of thought-provoking questions. Step One involves responding to these questions with a focus on the longest possible term for each one. It's important to acknowledge that the timeframe for your answers may differ from question to question, and that is perfectly acceptable. So, I want to reiterate: Your responses will naturally vary in terms of the future timeline you can envision, and this variance is entirely normal.

As we have discussed earlier in the program, some individuals are naturally inclined towards long-term thinking, while others lean more towards short-term perspectives. Many of us fall somewhere in between. The question-based process I'm about to guide you through is effective, and I have found that everyone can provide answers to the questions. As we progress through the questions, pause, and record your answer in your notebook. However, try not to dwell excessively on each question. Write down your responses as they emerge authentically and swiftly. You have invested considerable effort and preparation in previous chapters, which has primed your mind for this stage. Therefore, I urge you to capture your answers to the best of your ability, in a prompt and concise manner. As always, bullet points are perfectly suitable.

With each question, you have the freedom to approach it from a holistic life perspective or set specific milestones based on age, such as twenty-five, thirty, forty, fifty or sixty, or choose timeframes ranging from five to ten years into the future.

It may vary depending on the question, ranging from this year to next month. However, it's crucial for you to overcome what is easy or comfortable and challenge yourself. Your elastic band must stretch as we navigate through each of these questions. I particularly resonate with a quote from Susan Laurson Willig: "Limited expectations yield only limited results." Therefore, you must concentrate and commit your desires to writing. Dedicate yourself to focusing on the future and what you truly want, setting aside the current circumstances of your life. We will address those in Chapter 6. Right now, your focus should be on envisioning your desired future.

Keep in mind that your future can encompass questions as well. In Chapter 3, we prepared you to transform your questions into outcome statements. So, as we progress through this process, if the questions I present enable you to identify the questions you want answered, it's perfectly fine to initially jot them down and refine them into outcome statements later, using the techniques we taught you previously.

PERSONAL VISION

To proceed, please be ready with your notebook to record your answers to the questions I am about to present. Remember to pause each time. I will provide additional information and examples for each question, but it is up to you to articulate your own answers. As you respond to each question, keep your focus on the future you desire. What is the ultimate outcome you seek? What does it look like? Emphasise what you want. This has been stressed numerous times. Concentrate on what you want, even if it seems absent from your life at this moment, or even impossible to achieve. If it is what you want, you **must** note it.

For each of your answers, challenge yourself by repeatedly asking "why" five times in a row. This exercise will reveal your true desires. For instance, someone might say, "I want to be rich." Upon further enquiry, asking, "Why do I want to be rich?" might elicit responses such as, "I desire the freedom that comes with wealth", "I want to travel extensively", "I want to give generously to my church" or "I aspire to own homes within my means." Or all the above!

The true essence of wanting to be rich lies in the answers that reveal the underlying reasons behind it, such as providing quality education for one's children. Being rich is merely a means to achieve those genuine aspirations. As we progress through this process, it is crucial to contemplate why we desire what we have written down. Is there something deeper that you truly want? Through this journey, you might uncover those profound desires. Remember, don't dwell too long on a question. Capture what naturally emerges for you as you proceed.

Immerse yourself in your desired future and envision it as if it has already been realised. Visualize each question to the best of your ability. What if you have already achieved it? What does it look like?

Allow the picture to form vividly in your mind. Many of you may be visual thinkers, able to easily describe it in words. That's what you will write down. And remember the power of writing, as emphasised by David Ingvar. Have your notebook ready. Let's begin.

Question One: Consider the characteristics of the significant relationships you wish to have in your life. Think about the categories of people you see yourself spending time with. Is it family, colleagues, close friends or perhaps constantly forming new friendships because you genuinely enjoy it? How many close friends do you envision? What role do colleagues play in your imagined future? Describe the characteristics of these relationships. Are they characterised by high integrity and trust? Use words to paint a picture of the significant relationships you aspire to have in your life. Pause, answer the question and then ready yourself to continue.

Question Two: What does 'retirement' mean to you, and what will you be doing? Have you given retirement much thought? From my experience, I have observed that many retirees end up returning to work because, as they have shared with me, retirement was slowly extinguishing their spirit, if not 'killing' them. They had failed to plan adequately and hadn't gained clarity on what retirement truly entails. Sitting in front of the TV, pressing play and stop on a Netflix series, loses its charm over time, leaving people bored and feeling a sense of mental decline. They had not thoroughly contemplated what retirement meant to them.

Age is not a determining factor here. Regardless of your current age, what does retirement mean to you? For me, I'm happy to share that retirement entails having complete control over the work I engage in. I won't require payment for my efforts, although I may still receive compensation. Financially, I would have amassed enough wealth to continue pursuing meaningful work without the need for monetary compensation. In fact, I aspire to offer my services to those who cannot afford them currently. This is something I envision doing during my 'retirement'. I would have the freedom to choose how much I work, and I have a specific age in mind when I would like to embark on this path. Have you considered when you would like to commence living your own definition of retirement? Is it clear in your mind? When do you envision starting to live your version of retirement?

Question Three shifts your focus to the level of health you desire in the future. How do you see your overall health in terms of physical, mental and spiritual health? Envision a healthy version of yourself as clearly as possible. Looking into the future, what physical activities do you wish to engage in? Consider activities involving children, grandchildren, friends or partners. These activities should span as far into the future as you can envision, where maintaining good physical health is crucial. Additionally, I encourage you to contemplate your mental and spiritual well-being. What does your mental health look like? It could be something as simple as saying, "I want to be mentally healthy." Your spiritual health may relate to a religion, but you don't have to be religious to be spiritual. Envision your mental and spiritual health as far into the future as you can imagine.

Remember to 'pause' after each question and note your answers. If you find yourself stuck on a particular question, don't stress. The work you have done to this point will enable your answer to emerge. Trust the process.

Question Four delves into the role travel will play in your future. Is travel important to you? Do you envision it as part of your work or as a separate pursuit? Alternatively, perhaps you've already had your fill of travel and desire a more rooted existence, a sense of being 'local' wherever that may be. Therefore, consider the role travel would have in your future, and if it does play a part, reflect on why you would be travelling? If travel is a large part of your desired future, how will you be travelling? If flying, is economy what you see? Or first-class?

For instance, in my desired future, my twin brother resides in the United States with his family. I want to connect with them, allowing our families to forge a close physical bond. This is a significant reason why travel holds importance to me. I am crystal clear about the purpose behind my travels. I will also have business arrangements within the United States, meaning my travel will be able to be expensed to my business, which has a positive effect on my Wealth For Life element. Remember, all these elements of your life are interdependent.

Moving on to **Question Five**, where do you envision living? What defines 'home' for you? Is home a singular location, or do you envision multiple residences? In today's world, having more than one home is increasingly feasible. My twin brother, for instance, has diligently worked towards creating multiple homes in both the USA and Australia. Would you be shifting between various locations due to holiday destinations? Whether you own these locations or not, it can be a part of your travel experiences as well. Notice how these questions intertwine and build upon one another. Consider where you want to establish your living arrangements. It's worth noting that your answer to the first part of the question doesn't have to specify a particular location. It could involve living in different places for periods of two to three years, constantly on the move.

"I'm unsure of the specific locations, but what I truly desire is to continually experience different places throughout my life." That might be how you articulate it.

Moving on to **Question Six:** What significant accomplishments will you succeed in creating from this moment onward? Envision the major achievements you will have accomplished between now and the furthest point into the future you can imagine. These accomplishments can encompass a wide range, such as completing degrees or doctoral studies, establishing a successful business, securing a meaningful role within an organisation, being a bestselling author, being more in love with your life partner than the day you met or raising healthy children who positively contribute to society. Think broadly and consider achievements like publishing a book, releasing songs or engaging in acting. The possibilities are vast, and you have the power to define what constitutes an achievement. So, what will be the noteworthy accomplishments, in your perspective, that you will have successfully brought to life when you look far into the future?

Question Seven: On a personal level, how do you wish people to describe you across all your life roles? Consider how you want individuals to characterise you based on the various roles you occupy. What three key words or short phrases would consistently emerge in descriptions of you by different individuals, highlighting the person you are? For example, a phrase I'd like people to say about me, in our typical Australian vernacular, is, "He has a crack at life!" Imagine projecting these words consistently across all your life roles, envisioning as far into the future as possible.

Question Eight centres around the level of education you aim to achieve. As you envision the distant future, what is the highest level of formal education you aspire to attain? Disregard your current status and focus on your ideal educational attainment. What knowledge or expertise will you possess that you currently lack? It may seem peculiar to some when I pose the question, "What will you know that you don't yet know?" There are things you acknowledge you don't know. For instance, you may aspire to be an entrepreneur or build successful businesses, but you recognise that you lack the know-how at present. In such cases, you would state, "I will know how to build successful businesses." Similarly, in your professional journey, you might aspire to be recognised as a leader of high-performing teams, even though you currently lack the necessary skills. In this instance, you would express, "I will know how to create high-performing teams."

Cheryl, who we met earlier, stated, "I will know how to play a musical instrument and will perform in a band on stage in front of an audience."

Now, let's move on to **Question Nine**: What additional qualifications and competencies will you acquire over time? For instance, I have been a coach in my children's sports activities. As a result, I have gained competencies and qualifications in junior sports coaching for various sports, because I would not have been allowed to coach their teams if I did not gain the qualification and maintain it. If there's an area where I haven't obtained qualifications for my desired future, I would write down something like, "I will become a Certified Level One coach in {insert sport}."

Competencies can include playing musical instruments, singing, acting, painting, sculpting or similar skills that may not require official certifications but are demonstrable through your ability to perform them. You may have always desired to play a musical instrument but haven't learned how. If you could have what you desire in your envisioned future, you would be able to play an instrument, perform in concerts of different scales or engage in acting. These are the types of competencies or skills that I refer to, ones that may or may not require a formal certification, but require significant dedication to learning, that may be included in your response. If you could attain your desired future, what other qualifications and competencies would you acquire over time?

Moving on to **Question Ten**: What are the characteristics you seek in your work? Do you desire a high level of control or a low level of control? Some individuals aspire to be their own boss, while others prefer not to. What are your preferences? Do you wish to be an employee or self-employed? If self-employed, do you envision having a large company with many employees or just a few? Consider the characteristics you desire. Do you want to work in a small, medium or large organisation? Is travel an important aspect or not? Are you content with staying in one place? How close to your residence would you like your workplace to be? Do you prefer a lengthy commute or a short one? How will you commute? Reflect on your answers to these questions. Would you like a work role where you spend significant time away from home because you find fulfillment in that, or do you prefer a balance between travel and staying in one location? You may already have answers to these questions regarding the characteristics of your desired work.

Question Eleven delves into the type of work that will provide you with a sense of personal fulfillment. What kind of work will give you that feeling? For some individuals, it's the work they get paid for. Personally, I consider myself very fortunate to be in that position, and I aspire to continue experiencing it in the future. Therefore, I include doing this type of work, the work I find personally fulfilling, in my vision for the future, even though I already have it now. Remember, there may be aspects of your life that you wish to carry forward into your future.

It's fascinating how, as we progress through these questions, we discover that there are elements of our present that we still desire in our future. It's crucial to keep acknowledging and recording those aspects as well. Additionally, some of us excel in certain areas and receive substantial compensation for it. However, it may not necessarily bring us a sense of fulfillment. In such cases, we engage in volunteering or activities within our community or with our children, finding personal fulfillment through those avenues. Personal fulfillment can hold varying degrees of importance for different individuals. Now, consider this question: How important is personal fulfillment to you in relation to your future and the future you envision?

Moving on to **Question Twelve**: Reflecting on the previous eleven questions, how expensive do you anticipate your lifestyle to be? While you may not have precise figures, you should have a general idea. Will it be relatively expensive, moderately expensive or not very expensive? Do you envision being able to ride life's inevitable economic bumps that can be caused by the economy itself, or sudden health issues for yourself or a loved one? It's vital to comprehend the level of expense associated with your desired lifestyle because without that understanding, it becomes challenging to plan effectively for the future. So, let's address this question: Is your lifestyle expected to be expensive, moderately expensive or not very expensive? Whatever the answer may be, what matters is your desired lifestyle. It doesn't necessarily have to be excessively costly, but if your desired activities and pursuits involve significant expenses, then your lifestyle will be on the expensive side. It's crucial to have clarity in this regard because you can take the necessary action to create the wealth you require.

Now, let's proceed with your personal vision review. We have completed the initial stage of the process.

You now have the answers to all twelve questions. Take a moment to revisit your responses to each question, going back through questions one through twelve. You can go through them swiftly or take your time, it's entirely up to you. The goal is to ensure that your answers describe the desired outcome. If they don't, make the necessary modifications, ensuring that your answers are outcome focused. Starting your sentences with "I will" is a powerful way to express your intentions. Keep your focus on what you want, reminding yourself that these are the things you truly desire. If you're uncertain about certain aspects and whether they truly reflect your desires, use the technique of asking yourself "why" multiple times to delve deeper and uncover your genuine answers. Continually imagine your desired future as if it has already been accomplished and make any changes or updates that may be required based on this quick review.

Moving on to Step Two of the process, you now need to determine a timeframe for your plan. At this point, you have answered the twelve

PERSONAL VISION

questions, and the timeframes may vary. Some may be ten or twenty years into the future, while others may be as close as six months from now. Your task is to select a timeframe that you feel comfortable developing your whole-of-life plan around.

For example, I have a clear vision of my life in my eighties, even though it is a long way into the future. However, my current plan is based on a ten-year timeframe, and I have already worked through the first year of that plan. The vision section has undergone slight modifications, some strategies have changed, and my present reality has shifted towards my vision over time. Yet, because the initial elastic band of ten years is sufficiently long, that timeframe works for me.

For you, it could be ten, five or three years. If you are currently pursuing undergraduate or postgraduate studies, I encourage you to add one more year to the end of your studies as a minimum. So, if you were thinking about when you turn thirty or forty, consider adding '+1' to that, envisioning yourself at thirty-one, forty-one or fifty-one. Try to stretch that elastic band a little further than what you might initially be comfortable with because we need to challenge ourselves.

Now it's time for you to choose a timeframe for your plan. Once you have reviewed all your answers, you need to determine the timeframe we will be focusing on. After that, you will summarise the relevant elements from your answers into your Level One Chart Personal Vision Summary. If you are following the *Yes For Success* Online Course you will be able to download the relevant worksheets.

Let's consider an example to illustrate this process. Suppose you are currently thirty-one years old and have expressed a desire to retire by the age of sixty. This information would have been included in your previous answers regarding retirement. Now, when selecting the timeframe for your plan, you have decided to focus on a five-year period. Here's the catch: while you can envision your retirement at sixty, which is a difference of twenty-nine years, your plan will only encompass a five-year span.

To bridge this gap, you need to examine your overall desired income that you have articulated for retirement. Consider everything you have written about retirement, such as your aspiration to retire at sixty, travel extensively and support your children with their families. All these aspects need to be integrated into your comprehensive desired income.

Now, the question arises, "What outcome, if any, do you need to achieve within the next five years to embark on the journey of preparing yourself for your desired retirement at sixty?"

This becomes a focal point as you consider the steps and milestones necessary to fulfill your long-term vision while staying focused on the immediate future.

Let's consider an example to illustrate how this process works. Perhaps within your five-year plan, you want to explore self-managed superannuation funds in your country, like Australia. This entails understanding how you can generate wealth to support your retirement. During the next five years, this phase may primarily involve research, seeking the guidance of financial advisors and possibly accountants who specialise in this area. These experts can provide valuable advice and should be included in your Personal Success Team.

By focusing on this aspect within your five-year plan, you are addressing the response you previously wrote, which was centred on a retirement goal twenty-nine years into the future. The insights gained during Step Five become the key elements to modify and incorporate into your Level One Chart Personal Vision Summary.

PERSONAL VISION

You must repeat this process for each of the twelve questions. Take the time to review each question, either in dot point form or longhand format and write a summary that aligns with the timeframe you have selected for your plan. Your goal now is to complete your Level One Chart Personal Vision Summary, capturing the essence of your aspirations and desires.

Congratulations! You've done fantastic work. Just think about all the effort you put into identifying your fears, concerns, wants and desires. Now, you have a written Level One Chart Personal Vision Summary, along with comprehensive answers to the twelve questions. This summary serves as a focused guide for the remaining steps of your plan.

So, what's next? It's time to move on to Chapter 6: Present Reality, where we will return to the elastic band metaphor, and focus on everything that is currently happening in your life.

CHAPTER 6

PRESENT REALITY

"The first step toward change is awareness. The second step is acceptance."

Nathaniel Branden

This is Chapter 6: Present Reality. In this chapter, we will delve into the exploration and understanding of your current circumstances.

Unlike Chapter 5, where you followed a two-step process, this time you will follow a streamlined one-step process for assessing your present reality. You will focus on answering questions about your current situation without the need for modification. In Chapter 5, we worked on developing our personal vision by answering a series of questions and adjusting our responses to align with a specific timeframe. However, for your present reality, we will concentrate solely on what exists in your present reality.

The subsequent step after this will involve devising strategies that arise from the tension between your vision and your current reality. You continue to operate at the Level One Chart. During this phase, you will be concentrating on the Present Reality component at the bottom of the elastic band.

Your focus is simply on providing honest answers to the specific questions that will help you identify your present reality. It is crucial that you approach this task with complete transparency, acknowledging both the positive and negative aspects of yourself.

PRESENT REALITY

When it comes to self-assessment, we often have a natural bias. Some individuals may view things more positively than they actually are, while others may struggle to recognise their own strengths. To truly be honest with ourselves, we must be willing to confront what is good, what is bad and even what is less appealing. This requires a comprehensive evaluation. It can be helpful to seek the input of a trusted friend, partner or confidant, who can review your answers and provide their perspective. They may point out things that you have overlooked or challenge the accuracy of certain statements, allowing for a more balanced assessment.

Sharing your responses with someone you trust, who understands the context and respects the information you are sharing, is a wise idea. By doing so, you can gain additional insights and valuable feedback. Remember, if you truly desire to shape the future you aspire to, honesty and authenticity must serve as your starting point. This necessitates overcoming personal biases and considering multiple perspectives as you envision the future based on your present reality.

Please have your notebook ready and answer the following questions.

Question One: In your present reality, what aspects of your life do you perceive as positive at this moment? Take a moment to identify and appreciate the goodness in your life. Just like in Chapter 5, please pause, jot down your answer and then resume.

Question Two: What challenges are you currently facing? Reflect on different areas of your life such as relationships, work, study, finances and health. What are the obstacles or difficulties that you encounter? Take your time to explore and acknowledge these challenges.

Remember, these questions are intended to help you gain a deeper understanding of your present reality.

Question Three: Reflect on how you've been investing your time lately. Consider the past few months and contemplate what has been occupying most of your time. It could be that you've been devoted to caring for a loved one who has been unwell. Perhaps you're amid transitioning into university or embarking on a new job. Maybe you've recently experienced the joys of parenthood for the first time. Or you are recovering from a relationship breakdown or the loss of someone you loved. There are numerous possibilities that could account for your time, such as planning an exciting trip or holiday, or preparing to move into a new home, which involves sorting out your finances. Take a moment to assess where your time has been predominantly directed over the past few months.

Question Four: Consider the qualifications and special competencies that you possess. Qualifications are valuable assets that remain with you, regardless of when you attained them. Additionally, special competencies refer to unique skills or talents that may not necessarily be certified by a piece of paper. For example, you may showcase your singing abilities by participating in your church choir, or perhaps you have a talent for playing a musical instrument, acting or engaging in drama-related activities. Another special competency could be excelling as a local-level athlete, earning numerous trophies and accomplishments in various sports. Reflect on both your formal qualifications and these exceptional abilities that set you apart.

Question Five: Explore the hobbies that captivate your interest and bring you joy. Consider the activities that ignite your passion. It might be helpful to refer to your response in Chapter 4: Passion and recollect what you wrote there. Evaluate the level of presence your passion currently holds in your life. For instance, I am deeply passionate about supporting the Western Bulldogs in the Australian Football League.

PRESENT REALITY

What stirs your enthusiasm? Perhaps your passion lies in cherishing moments with your family, creating joyful experiences with your children. Or maybe you find exhilaration in embarking on motorcycle rides alongside your friends. Some may be passionate about their work, like me, where I derive fulfillment from teaching individuals how to plan for personal success and achieve greatness. What about you? What sparks your passion, and to what extent does it manifest in your life?

Question Six: Reflect on the state of your significant relationships. Take a moment to jot down the names of individuals whom you consider holding pivotal roles in your life. Begin with your family, partner, close friends and colleagues, and observe the size of your list. If you have more than twenty names, it's likely more than sufficient; most people tend to have around ten key relationships, but it could be as few as five. Identify the key relationships you share with these individuals. Now, employ a simple rating system: place a '+' next to their name if you are highly confident that the relationship is currently in a positive state. If you're unsure about the status, wondering how they perceive the relationship, you may opt for a '?'. Conversely, if you feel certain that the relationship is not as satisfactory as you desire, use a '–' symbol. Once again, compile a list of the significant relationships in your life and employ the symbols '+' (positive), '?' (uncertain), or '–' (in need of improvement) to assess their current status.

Question Seven: Assessing Your Financial Landscape. In the quest to understand your financial standing, it becomes imperative to delve into the depths of your wealth and assets. How do you calculate your net worth? How familiar are you with the concept of 'assets minus liabilities'? Moreover, do these terms resonate with you, or do they baffle your mind? To truly comprehend the intricacies of wealth and finance, it is vital to grasp their underlying mechanisms.

Let us probe further into your monetary affairs. Is your credit card a testament to your financial prudence? Or do you find yourself ensnared in the web of interest payments? Does your mobile phone bill align with your prearranged arrangements, or do you frequently find yourself surpassing the allocated limits? These seemingly trivial details offer insightful clues about your present status in terms of wealth and financial management.

Consider this; if your aspirations encompass becoming an entrepreneur and steering businesses to success, do you possess the fundamental knowledge of structuring a business, particularly from an accounting and marketing standpoint? Familiarity with these domains hold tremendous value. Therefore, it is worth contemplating your expertise in this realm.

As you navigate the elements of wealth and finance, there are numerous factors deserving of your attention. Evaluating your current financial and wealth status entails introspection into these matters. How is your cash-flow? Cash-flow is king and understanding this aspect of finance and wealth is essential. How well do you understand this concept now?

Question Eight: Nurturing Your Health and Well-being. In the pursuit of a prosperous and fulfilling life, it is vital to assess your current state of health and fitness. How would you describe your well-being? Do you make regular visits to the doctor, prioritising your overall wellness? Equally important is comprehending the intricacies of your body's functioning, both in terms of physical activity and nutrition. What is your dietary regimen like? How would you define your understanding of diet and nutrition? It is worth contemplating your knowledge in this realm.

Furthermore, understanding the significance of physical activity and its impact on your health holds great value. Do you grasp the connection between exercise and well-being? How well-versed are you in this domain? Do you have a trusted individual within your Personal

Success Team who supports you in gaining the necessary knowledge and understanding in these areas?

Take a moment to reflect on your habits. Are there any habits you are aware of that contribute to an unhealthy lifestyle? Despite being cognisant of their adverse effects, do you find yourself repeatedly engaging in these habits? Additionally, how well-versed are you in the realm of sleep? Do you possess knowledge of your sleep cycles and understand when it is most beneficial for you to rest? For instance, I have discovered that, to the best of my ability, being asleep between the hours of 2 a.m. and 5 a.m. suits me best. I can function with relatively low amounts of sleep for short durations. However, deviating from this pattern, even for a single night, leaves me feeling jet-lagged for three days as I struggle to readjust.

As you embark on the journey towards holistic well-being, it is imperative to examine your health and fitness status. By developing a deep understanding of your body and cultivating healthy habits, you pave the way for a vibrant and prosperous life.

Throughout my personal journey, I have come to appreciate the paramount importance of quality sleep. I have made it a priority to ensure that I am soundly asleep during a specific window of time. Like many individuals, I generally require around seven hours of sleep for optimal functioning. However, I have also discovered that there are periods when I can manage with less. How well do you understand your own sleep patterns and needs? Exploring this realm can shed light on a crucial aspect of your well-being.

Mental health, an integral component of overall wellness, also warrants your attention. How do you nurture your mental well-being? Do you have practices in place that promote mental clarity and resilience? Assessing your mental health status becomes crucial. What have you learned about mental health, and how do you gauge its well-being?

How do you manage your self-talk? The way you talk to yourself affects your actions, which in turn affects your attitude.

Spiritual health, encompassing various aspects of personal belief and connectedness, holds significance as well. Regardless of whether spirituality aligns with religious frameworks, it remains a key element of self-reflection. What is your present spiritual stance? How are you currently nurturing your spiritual well-being? Reflecting upon these questions brings clarity to your spiritual dimension.

Another vital aspect to consider is the need for rejuvenation through holidays and breaks. How do you approach this? Do you plan and book holidays in advance or take them spontaneously? Assessing your current reality in terms of holidaying and re-energising helps you gauge your well-being. Have you recently enjoyed a holiday? When was your last retreat? Are there any upcoming plans in place, including bookings and payments? Delving into these details illuminates your status in relation to health and fitness.

To embark on a path of holistic well-being, it is essential to reflect upon your health and fitness status. By cultivating an understanding of your sleep patterns, mental health, spiritual nourishment and the rejuvenation you seek, you set the foundation for a balanced and fulfilling life.

Question Nine: Reflecting on Your Lifelong Triumphs. As you embark on the journey of personal growth, it is essential to acknowledge and celebrate the achievements you have accomplished thus far. Take a moment to contemplate your life's milestones. What are the triumphs that hold a special place in your heart? These achievements are a testament to your capabilities and character, and they can never be taken away from you. Perhaps you were the esteemed 'Dux' at your high school, an accomplishment from years gone by that still shines brightly. Maybe you have earned degrees, embraced the journey of parenthood, amassed wealth or orchestrated the establishment of multiple successful businesses. What achievements have you created in your life? Remember, you define what constitutes an achievement, so it is up to you to define and appreciate these personal victories. Take the time to jot them down, recognising their enduring significance.

Question Ten: Nurturing Meaningful Networks. Another crucial aspect of personal success lies in the strength and quality of your networks. Assessing the status of your connections allows you to gauge the support and growth opportunities available to you. Consider the various spheres of your life, local, career and online networks. Evaluate the vitality of your community connections, the presence of mentor figures, and even your affiliations within your church, sports or creative communities. How active are your networks? Do they foster a sense of closeness and collaboration? Have you recently extended your support to someone within your network? Your network reflects your net worth. Who are you spending time with? Who do you listen to? Are they successful? Everyone has a right to an opinion. But all opinions are not equal. How selective are you about who you listen to? What is your honest answer? These enquiries offer valuable insight into the status of your networks.

Nurturing mentor relationships can prove particularly influential. Are there individuals in your life who provide guidance, wisdom, and support? Likewise, are you utilising your own knowledge and experiences to mentor others? Embracing the reciprocal nature of mentorship strengthens your personal growth and contributes to the growth of those around you. When you mentor someone else you must be clear about what you think, otherwise you can't provide sage advice when it is requested. Becoming a mentor trains you to clarify what you really believe about important topics. And becoming a mentor challenges you to be succinct with how you explain what you believe, otherwise your mentee is not going to understand you. As

Einstein reportedly said, simplicity sits at the far side of complexity. Again, what role is mentoring playing in your life, today?

Reflect upon these questions. Celebrate your achievements, both big and small, recognising the unique path you have travelled. Assess the status of your networks, nurturing connections that foster support and growth. By embracing your achievements and cultivating meaningful relationships, you pave the way for continued personal success.

Question Eleven: Evaluating Your Career Path. Examining the current status of your career is a pivotal step towards personal success. Take a moment to reflect on your work experiences thus far. Have you engaged in part-time or full-time employment? What roles have you taken on during your professional journey? As you ponder these questions, consider the employability skills you have developed over time.

Employability skills encompass a range of valuable competencies, such as problem-solving, effective communication, teamwork, planning and organisation, service excellence, as well as initiative and enterprise. Reflect on how you have demonstrated these skills through your past work experiences. What specific examples can you provide that highlight your proficiency in these areas?

Volunteering also plays a significant role in shaping one's professional journey. If you have worked before, consider the impact that volunteering has had on your life. For those who have never had formal work experience, volunteering can offer valuable opportunities to develop skills, gain exposure to different environments and showcase your commitment to making a positive impact.

It is not uncommon for individuals, particularly university students and postgraduate scholars, to prioritise studies to the point of neglecting work experiences. However, it is essential to recognise that lacking work experience may pose challenges when seeking future employment.

PRESENT REALITY

Demonstrating employability skills becomes crucial in showcasing your value to potential employers. Take stock of your current status in this regard. Have you been actively developing your employability skills through various avenues?

Take the time to evaluate your career trajectory, considering both work and volunteering experiences. By recognising the employability skills you possess and seeking opportunities to further develop them, you position yourself as a desirable candidate in the eyes of employers.

Honestly, there is no such thing as 'just' a part-time or permanent job. Whether you find yourself working as a waitress, at a local fast-food establishment, a convenience store or a petrol station, these roles hold immense value. Dismissing them as insignificant would be a disservice to your personal and professional growth. Each of these jobs provides an opportunity, at the very minimum, to develop essential employability skills.

Consider the skills you cultivate in these roles: problem-solving, effective communication, teamwork, planning and organisation, and continuous learning. Even in seemingly modest positions, there are technologies to learn, systems to navigate and tasks that require problem-solving. These experiences are not to be underestimated; they hold relevance for your future endeavours.

Awareness is key. Recognise the value of these jobs and be mindful of the skills you are honing along the way. Capture stories and examples that illustrate your growth and the application of these employability skills. In my comprehensive *Say Yes for Career Success* program, the first online program I created, I dedicated modules to guide people in understanding and harnessing their employability skills. The course was an enhancement to my first book *What Really Matters for Young Professionals! How to Master 15 Practices to Accelerate Your Career*.

My first job that I got myself was when I was ten years old. I arose at 5 a.m. and completed a paper round six days per week, riding more than 10 kilometres to finish my round. I earned AUD$11.26 per week. It is funny the things you remember! I had to deliver those papers in rain, hail and sunshine. I rode through spider webs and had spiders on my face! I had wild dogs chase me. I was scared at times. It was dark, cold and wet in the middle of winter. The wind nearly blew me backwards as I rode over a major bridge. I cried at times because it was so cold, wet and windy and I thought my heart would pound out of my chest as I pushed down on the pedals to ride over the bridge, against winter's south westerly wind.

I also won! A lot. I challenged myself to deliver the papers, with either hand, by folding them and placing them in the letterbox without stopping my bike. I challenged myself to deliver all the papers properly and complete the round faster. On a Saturday morning, two of the papers, *The Age* and *The Australian*, were multiple times bigger than their weekday size. It wasn't possible to carry all the papers in one effort. So, I had to go back to the newsagency partway through the round to refill my bags. I challenged myself to identify the optimal spot in my round to go and refill my bags. I got to make the decision for myself and work out what worked best. And I 'won' my little competition with myself to complete my round faster. A Personal Best, if you like! I did this paper round for four years.

By the age of fourteen, I was a working 'machine'. This is when I got my first 'proper' job, working on the front counter at our local McDonald's restaurant. It was 1983 and Australia had become McDonald's most successful market, per capita, in the world. I was recruited to work on the front counter, which was different to what had been happening up until my appointment. At that time, girls and women worked out the front. Boys and men worked out the back in the kitchen.

PRESENT REALITY

I remember the interview. It was conducted in one of the booths in the restaurant. At the end of the interview, Frank (I wish I could recall his surname) told me I was successful and would be working out the front, the first male recruited to do so. He asked if I was happy to take some advice from him. I thought to myself, *Sure, Frank. You're my new boss. You can tell me the sun comes up in the west if you like. I'll listen!*

Frank said, "Gary, you have been successful in this interview. Remember, every time you turn up for a shift, you are being interviewed for your next opportunity."

I don't know how I understood what Frank meant. But I did. He was saying, always turn up and do your best. If you do your best, opportunities will come your way.

I have carried Frank's advice with me my entire life and it has paid off in spadefuls! Thank you, Frank.

When I first started working on the front counter, we had notepads where we wrote down customer orders, then had to manually add up the total for their food and drinks. Our store was the second drive-thru service in Australia. Cars drove up to the window and we took their order with the notepad, just as we did at the restaurant counter. It was the same process, except the people remained in their car.

Within the first year, technology arrived. We got computer registers and no longer had to use maths to add up the customer order. We got a new process for the drive-thru service with speakers and microphones. A lot changed in the three years I worked at McDonald's.

Would it be appropriate to say those two jobs were 'just' jobs? Would it be appropriate to say that I didn't learn anything from those jobs for my career? I have three degrees. I promise you, those two jobs taught me just as much, possibly even more, than two of my three degrees taught me about work and success.

Never underestimate any job. Every job has value for your career. First, you have to have the mindset to 'see' the benefits. What are the lifelong lessons you have learned from the work you have done?

Question Twelve: Bridging the Gap between Vision and Reality. Now, it's time to retrieve your Level One Chart Personal Vision Summary, which you created at the end of Chapter 5. Ensure you have your notes in front of you as we delve into aligning your present reality with your envisioned future. Take a moment to review each point listed in your Level One Chart Personal Vision Summary.

Here's what we're aiming for; if there is no corresponding point in your present reality for what you have written in your Level One Chart Personal Vision Summary, this is the perfect opportunity to address it. Your Level One Chart Personal Vision Summary outlines what you desire for your future, specifying time-based and timeframe-specific goals. It may include aspirations regarding retirement, wealth, travel and more.

As we progress through the previous eleven questions exploring your present reality, you may find that certain points from your Level One Chart Personal Vision Summary have not yet been addressed. This is where you can bridge the gap. Take a moment to write down your current status or situation for each point that has not been captured in the previous questions. By doing so, you ensure that your Present Reality Summary perfectly correlates with what you have articulated in your Level One Chart Personal Vision Summary.

For example, imagine you have a dot point in your Level One Chart Personal Vision Summary that says, "I will take my family on an extended overseas holiday every year."

Yet, in your Present Reality responses you haven't mentioned anything about your current status as it relates to family holidays. This may be because you don't yet have a family, so it slipped your mind. In

PRESENT REALITY

this instance, you may write something like, "I have been on three overseas trips to Asia, New Zealand and Europe with different groups of friends. These trips have created a desire for regular overseas trips for holiday purposes."

This exercise serves as an opportunity to identify areas where your present reality may need adjustment or alignment with your envisioned future. It allows you to actively work towards closing the gap between your aspirations and your current situation. Take the time to complete this step, ensuring that your present reality becomes a true reflection of your personal vision.

As you progress through this chapter, remember that your Level One Chart Personal Vision Summary is a guiding light, helping you navigate towards your desired future. It acts as a magnet drawing you towards your future. Please stop now and complete this activity.

Okay, fantastic job! You have successfully reached the bottom of your elastic band for your Level One Chart. This signifies a significant milestone in your personal plan for success, encompassing your entire life journey.

Now, what lies ahead? Let's turn our attention to Chapter 7, where we delve into Identify Strategies. Here, we will focus on the crucial steps you need to take to bridge the gap between your present reality and your personal vision. This is an exciting phase of your journey, as you begin charting the course that will lead you towards the realisation of your aspirations.

Leading up to this point, remember to maintain an unwavering commitment to learning and personal growth. Embrace the mindset of continuous improvement and strive to be the best version of yourself in all that you do. Your dedication to ongoing development will serve as a strong foundation for the upcoming phases of your journey.

As we embark on Chapter 7 and dive into the realm of identifying strategies, remain open to the possibilities that lie ahead. Stay enthusiastic, motivated and ready to take inspired action. Your personal plan for success is within reach, and each step you take brings you closer to turning your vision into reality.

Continue your journey with a sense of purpose, knowing that every effort you invest will propel you towards the life you envision.

IDENTIFY STRATEGIES

"Strategy without tactics is the slowest route to victory. Tactics without strategy is the noise before defeat."

Sun Tzu

It brings me immense joy to guide you through Chapter 7: Identify Strategies. This is the stage where you uncover the steps required to propel you from your present reality towards your personal vision. It's an exhilarating phase, as you delve into the intricate details of charting your path towards the future you desire, conquering your fears and uncertainties, and reclaiming control over your life.

Now, it's time to embark on the heart of the elastic band metaphor, your strategies that will bridge the gap between your present reality and your envisioned future. While you continue operating at the Level One Chart, this chapter will provide a comprehensive guide on how to identify the high-level strategies that you can turn into actionable plans and Chapter 8. This detailed process empowers you to take charge of your life, craft your success and conquer any lingering apprehensions about what lies ahead.

By identifying your strategies now, you ensure that you remain firmly in the driver's seat, equipped with the precise actions needed to propel you along your journey. You cultivate a deep understanding of how to navigate challenges, staying focused and on track to achieve your desired outcomes. Your strategies become your guiding light, leading you towards success while dispelling any lingering doubts.

In our journey towards personal success, it's time for a shift in focus. You move away from the encompassing whole-of-life level of your vision and shift your attention towards the question, "What steps will propel me forward?" As you delve into this stage, let us recall the insightful second illustration by Jock McLeish, which emphasises the importance of balance as you progress. However, it's crucial to acknowledge that each segment of the wheel holds different significance at various stages of your life.

The six vital strategies are:

1. Self-Awareness
2. Fitness and Health
3. Learn for Success
4. Wealth for Life
5. Career Options
6. Relationships Matter

You are unique, with your own set of circumstances. Therefore, different parts of the wheel will come into sharper focus for each of you. This diversity is perfectly acceptable and expected. As you embark on identifying strategies, it is essential to aim for at least one actionable strategy in each of the six key areas that I call the 'Six Vital Strategies'.

While one area of your life might require more attention, necessitating five, six or even ten strategies, it is equally important not to neglect the other areas. You mustn't risk falling into the trap represented by the individual on the left-hand side of the illustration, who focused solely on three parts of the wheel, neglecting the other three. Such an approach would leave you with an incomplete wheel, hindering your progress towards personal success.

IDENTIFY STRATEGIES

Therefore, as you identify your strategies, ensure that you allocate sufficient resources and effort to maintain progress in all areas. By doing so, you safeguard against imbalance and maintain a robust foundation for your journey ahead. Let us learn from this valuable metaphor and forge ahead with determination, embracing the power of strategic focus and balance.

Remember, the key to success lies not only in addressing crucial areas but also in maintaining a holistic approach. Together, I will guide you as you navigate this transformative process, armed with actionable strategies that encompass every facet of your life.

Since our focus lies primarily on actively engaging with life, it is imperative to employ action-oriented language. You need to employ 'doing' words, or formulate statements that capture the essence of doing, when articulating your intentions. While the list I provide is by no means exhaustive, it serves as a starting point, offering you a range of words to consider. These words can be used independently, or as the beginning or middle of a sentence, as you describe the steps you will take to bridge the gap between your present and your envisioned future.

Ensure you have your Level One Chart Personal Vision Summary and Present Reality Summary within reach as you embark on this process. It may require a bit of space, but ideally, you should be able to view both documents simultaneously. The purpose behind this is to jot down the actions you will take to bridge the gap between your Present Reality and your Level One Chart Personal Vision Summary.

When considering the strategies for each of the six vital areas, you will likely find words such as 'research' or 'explore' to be of great significance. In fact, it's highly probable that researching or exploring will be essential components within nearly every strategy. These actions involve seeking out information and uncovering new insights. So, if you find yourself struggling to formulate a strategy for a specific vital area, such as relationships, consider the value of research or exploration.

Additionally, verbs like 'join' or 'commence' may prove useful. Starting something new, either by joining an endeavour or commencing a project, can be instrumental in achieving your goals. These verbs offer a means to initiate action within your various strategies.

'Read' is an action-oriented word, indicating the need to seek out information and broaden your knowledge. It plays a vital role in acquiring necessary insights. Similarly, 'recruit' can be relevant when it comes to expanding your social connections or engaging in other forms of recruitment, such as cultivating a new member of your Personal Success Team.

Furthermore, 'start' or 'complete' may be necessary in certain instances. If there are unfinished tasks or projects that hinder your progress, it becomes crucial to see them through to completion. Alternatively, if you often find yourself procrastinating, it may be essential to take that first step and initiate action, regardless of the specific topic or task at hand.

By employing these carefully chosen words, I will guide you through the exploration of the six vital strategies, offering you the tools to shape your path towards success.

There may come a time when you need to 'identify' certain aspects of yourself, others or various facets of your life. Perhaps you need to pinpoint areas for improvement or gain a deeper understanding of certain elements. Setting targets is another crucial step, one that involves working towards specific goals. Consider setting educational standards or grade levels as you progress through your formal education—a tangible target to strive for.

Learning is an essential part of growth. You might need to acquire new skills, such as playing the guitar or singing. Embracing the process of learning opens up possibilities and expands your horizons. On the other hand, there are instances where you must possess the courage to 'quit'. It's important to remember that successful individuals excel at relinquishing activities or habits that hinder their progress. For example, in the realm of health, you might need to let go of behaviours that are detrimental. Recognising that your present reality includes unhealthy practices while your personal vision emphasises well-being, a shift is imperative. 'Quit' becomes a potent word; one that captures the essence of change and growth. Quitting something that isn't contributing to your success is smart as it creates the time and space for the new activities you need to undertake to create the life you want.

Perhaps there are things you aim to 'gain' along this journey. It could be information, insights or even weight, depending on your motivations and goals. These verbs serve as tools to support you throughout this process.

Additionally, you might find it necessary to 'repair' a relationship or 'fix' an issue at work. These words can be instrumental in addressing challenges as you navigate your vital strategies. Furthermore, 'travel' or 'visit' might be actions you consider incorporating into your plans.

Vital Strategy One: Self-Awareness

Now, let's delve into **Vital Strategy One: Self-Awareness**. This strategy centres around understanding and honouring your own identity. When you possess clarity about who you truly are, you gain the ability to make sound decisions at the right moments, driven by the right reasons. This alignment allows you to become the person you aspire to be and to shape the future you desire.

Throughout each of the six vital strategies, I will provide you with concise definitions, just as I have done for 'self-awareness.' Additionally, I will offer example strategies to guide you further along this transformative journey.

In presenting these examples, I aim to stimulate your thinking and ignite your imagination. It is important to note that these examples are not prescriptive; they merely serve as prompts to help you generate your own strategies. You have the freedom to choose whether to adopt any of these suggestions. Ultimately, this is your plan, and your unique and personal journey.

By offering these examples for each of the six vital strategies, my intention is to activate your mind and inspire your thought process. Following each explanation, I encourage you to pause, and use your notebook to list your answer. Take your time to explore and identify the vital strategies that resonate with you. Now, let's begin this transformative process.

Let's explore potential strategies for Vital Strategy One: Self-Awareness. One approach is to enhance your personal success plan by creating Level Two Charts for each strategy you have identified at the Level One Chart. In Chapter 8, following this chapter, I will guide you through the process of creating your Level Two Charts. It is worth noting that dedicating time to complete a Level Two Chart for many of the strategies you identify for each of the six vital strategies is a crucial step. While not all your vital strategies will require a Level Two Chart, many of them will.

This commitment is essential if you truly aspire to take charge of creating the success you desire. To be clear, I am recommending that you identify a strategy as part of Vital Strategy One: Self-Awareness, to create Level Two Charts for all the strategies you identify across the six vital strategies. This may ultimately be ten, twenty, thirty or more

IDENTIFY STRATEGIES

Level Two Support Charts. After a while, you will become a master at creating them and each one will give you clarity about the actions you need to take to create the outcomes and fulfillment you desire. Level Two Charts will be explained in detail in Chapter 8.

Another strategy involves identifying and recruiting individuals to be a part of your Personal Success Team. We have previously discussed the concept of your Personal Success Team in Chapter 2. Now is the perfect opportunity to document this intention and state it clearly: "I am committed to creating my personal success team and identifying and recruiting individuals to join that team."

Moreover, you may choose to identify those individuals for whom you serve as a member of their personal success team. Include this as a strategy by listing their names and affirming your commitment: "I am dedicated to being a valuable member of the personal success team for these individuals."

Consider the strategy of exploring and understanding your personality, strengths, and weaknesses. Engaging in assessments and self-reflection can provide valuable insights into who you truly are.

In the realm of self-discovery, there are various tools at our disposal. The Myers-Briggs assessment, DISC analysis, Wave methodology, What Makes People Tick, Talent Predix and more all provide valuable insights into your nature. If you have completed these assessments in the past, your strategy may be to find them and review them for insights. It is possible for your personality preferences to change over time, which may suggest it is time to complete an assessment as part of one of your strategies.

An essential aspect of personal success lies in comprehending how your energy operates. My eBook *Energy for Success* has shed light on this matter. This section of your plan is an ideal spot to document your strategy to implement your OTM Personal Cycle for Success.

Your strategy may look something like, "I shall set my personal cycle for success in motion. I will ensure its effectiveness by developing a heightened awareness of it over the next twelve months. Through refinement, I aim to establish my own OTM Personal Cycle for Success, guaranteeing that I possess the necessary energy for achieving my goals. This proactive approach will prevent me from succumbing to procrastination when confronted with vital tasks, actions and steps crucial to manifesting the future I desire."

In the pursuit of a fulfilling career, many individuals aspire to take on leadership roles. However, the desire for leadership cannot remain confined to mere aspirations. To truly understand the essence of leadership, one must venture out and immerse oneself in leadership experiences. Theoretical pondering alone falls short; it is through active engagement that you truly become a leader. This deliberate approach intertwines with self-awareness, as we shall soon discover. It's worth noting that the strategies we discuss are interconnected, supporting and complementing each other. Some strategies can even find their place in multiple vital strategic categories. For instance, seeking opportunities to lead could also be considered within the realm of 'career'. However, I include it here in Vital Strategy One: Self-Awareness because experiencing leadership firsthand allows you to gauge your abilities and determine whether it is a role you can effectively undertake. Thus, seeking opportunities to lead becomes a conscious and purposeful strategy that propels you towards the desired success you envision.

A final strategy to consider is deliberately feeding your mind material that 'primes' it for whatever you are about to do. I deliberately feed my mind with material that is focused and positive before I do something important. When I am driving to deliver a program for a client, I always listen to something positive and constructive that will 'prime' my mind for the activity I am about to undertake. If I am about to have a challenging conversation, I will prime my mind with material on

IDENTIFY STRATEGIES

listening and conversation techniques. Given neuroscience teaches us that we continue to be a fundamentally emotional, irrational species, and our brains are attracted to negativity like Velcro, it is a powerful technique to deliberately 'prime' your mind for positivity before you do something important. If you lead a team, what are you using to prime your mind before a team meeting or your individual meetings? This strategy works; please consider it.

Now is the ideal moment to pause and reflect. Take this opportunity to document at least one strategy for self-awareness in your notebook, though feel free to jot down more if necessary. These strategies serve as stepping stones, bridging the gap between your current reality and the summation of your personal vision.

Vital Strategy Two: Fitness and Health

In this section, we'll explore how physical, mental and spiritual well-being contribute to your overall success. As you review your Level One Chart Personal Vision Summary and Present Reality, take note of any gaps you identify in your physical, mental and spiritual health. These gaps will serve as opportunities for growth and improvement.

Consider implementing the following strategies to help you align with your Level One Chart Personal Vision Summary:

1. Research and adopt a healthier diet: Take the time to explore and implement dietary changes that promote optimal health. A well-nourished body is the foundation for sustained success.
2. Establish a physical exercise/activity schedule: Engage in regular physical activity that suits your preferences and lifestyle. Whether it's going for a run, joining a fitness class or finding joy

in outdoor activities, prioritising regular exercise will enhance your overall well-being.

3. Schedule routine health checks: Make it a habit to book and attend regular health check-ups. For men in particular, this step is crucial, as many tend to neglect this aspect of self-care. Consider visiting different health professionals, such as psychologists or specialists, to ensure a comprehensive check-up.

4. Cultivate your mental and spiritual health: Deliberately focus on activities that contribute to your mental and spiritual well-being. This could involve practising meditation, exploring literature that nourishes your mind, or engaging in activities that bring you inner peace and fulfillment.

5. Plan and pay for holidays in advance: Take the proactive step of booking and paying for your holidays well in advance. By doing so, you create an opportunity to rest, relax and rejuvenate. Personally, I have found this strategy immensely valuable since the late 1990s. Michelle and I make it a tradition to book our holidays for the upcoming year right after the Christmas period. This not only gives us something to look forward to but also ensures that we prioritise time for rest and renewal.

Remember, incorporating these strategies into your life will not only prevent burnout but also provide you with the energy and vitality needed to achieve exceptional results. Take charge of your fitness and health and unlock your full potential for success.

Example: In my case, I already have my next holiday booked to visit my twin brother and his family in the USA, while I am travelling there for business. Have you already scheduled yours? This could be a strategy you consider implementing. Additionally, setting goals that require physical activity can be beneficial. For many years I aimed to complete at least one marathon. Michelle completed four 100-kilometre Oxfam

IDENTIFY STRATEGIES

Trailwalker events. This year, due to having had my second hip replacement (caused by a congenital issue unrelated to my marathon running) my aim was to return to a minimum of 10,000 steps per day within six weeks of the surgery, and then progress that to 15,000 steps. Both have been achieved and my current goal is to walk at least 35 kilometres per week (which I am succeeding at completing each week).

Setting ambitious goals forces you to engage in the necessary training and keeps you motivated. Having physical goals that demand action can be an effective strategy to keep you active and moving towards success. These are just a few examples of the fitness and health strategies you can explore.

In terms of my mental and spiritual health I researched an app that provides a source of information and activities that serve both my mental and spiritual health. Some of the lessons and meditations are up to thirty minutes, while many are as little as a few minutes. These practices, in hand with journalling my big goals and an example of magic every day, help maintain my mental and spiritual health.

Use your notebook and record your strategies for this vital strategy. Don't worry if you don't know exactly how you will bring those strategies to life. You will learn that step in Chapter 8.

Vital Strategy Three: Learn for Success

Learning is an essential component of survival and creating success. Just as you need to eat, drink and breathe, you must continually discover and stretch your abilities through learning. In fact, I go as far as to say that learning is equivalent to oxygen. Without it, you will not survive. Research is a vital activity that supports the development of your vital strategies and guides you towards the right actions for achieving the success you desire. Let's delve into some 'learn for success' strategies:

1. Research and explore your passions: Consider incorporating this strategy into your plan if you haven't already addressed it in Vital Strategy One: Self-Awareness. Discovering your passions fuels your motivation and enhances your overall success.
2. Implement the necessary learning for each vital strategy: As we have observed, each strategy requires its own learning process. If you haven't assigned specific learning tasks to each strategy, you can consolidate them under this vital strategy. This reinforces the importance of continuous learning and ensures you don't overlook any essential knowledge or skills.
3. Establish educational standards: If you are currently engaged in formal education, set clear standards for yourself. Define the level of achievement you aim to reach and establish milestones along the way to monitor your progress.

Remember, learning is an ongoing journey that supports your path to success. Embrace these 'learn for success' strategies and cultivate a thirst for knowledge as you navigate towards your desired future.

Setting a standard for your formal education is just as crucial as setting physical goals within the fitness and health vital strategy. It involves learning about employability skills and crafting compelling stories that showcase how you have applied those skills in real-life situations.

Another aspect to consider is committing to other important qualifications and competencies that align with your personal vision. This could involve pursuing certifications in specific areas, such as becoming qualified as a junior sports coach or developing proficiency in playing a musical instrument, singing, dancing or any other skill that resonates with you.

Furthermore, establishing deliberate learning habits is key. Allow me to share an anecdote from my own experience. In the year 2000, I had the privilege of meeting Dr Betty Siegel, the longest-serving female president in the public university system in the USA at that time. During her presentation, she recounted a discussion she had with one of her mentors when she was around thirty-five years old. The mentor emphasised the importance of deliberate learning habits for leadership and success. While Betty hadn't studied leadership, she had a desire to become a senior leader in a university. Her mentor recommended she dedicate ten minutes per day to being a 'student of leadership'. While this doesn't seem a lot of time, Betty practised this concept for nearly forty years. As she said, in her first year she realised how much she had studied in a single year, despite being extremely busy raising her family and progressing her career. Then, suddenly five years had passed. She continued with this practice of studying leadership for ten minutes per day. Her career had skyrocketed, and she had indeed become a president of a university. But she didn't become complacent. She kept learning. She maintained the practice. She did the smart, hard work, for decades! The cumulative effect of studying and then practising what she was learning resulted in her becoming the longest-serving female president of a university in the United States by the time of her retirement.

And as she shared this story, Betty reminded us that in today's digital age, we have an abundance of resources at our disposal—TED.com, blogs, books, audiobooks, podcasts, YouTube videos, the list goes on and on and on. If you want to learn a subject, the material is available if you are prepared to dedicate time and effort to it. Ten minutes per day! This is doable! The opposite is also true. There are a multitude of digital options that feed Resistance, drawing you away from spending time and investing in your development. Entertainment has never been easier. But it won't create the success, life harmony and fulfillment you desire. Imagine trading ten minutes of digital entertainment, scrolling

TikTok, for example, for learning a subject important to your future. Maybe this is a strategy you could employ?

This powerful strategy—a habit of lifelong learning—has had a profound impact on my journey as well. I encourage you to embrace it. Consider dedicating just ten minutes each day to explore and deepen your knowledge in areas that align with your goals and aspirations. By consistently investing this time in your personal growth, you will be amazed at the progress you can make over time.

Trade entertainment time for learning time. If you did an inventory on your time, you would see just how much time you have available to invest in your learning. I promise you. It isn't that you don't have time, it is how you choose to use your time that makes all the difference.

Don't be surprised when you discover you have much more than ten minutes per day that you could trade from entertainment time to learning time.

I have never watched *Game of Thrones*. I know it was huge. I know people loved it. I promise you; it has made zero difference to my life for having NOT watched it. Instead, I put the same time I would have been sitting and watching *Game of Thrones* into my learning. You can too!

Please, if you have watched every episode of *Game of Thrones*, don't take this as a personal attack. I am using that series as the example because it was so popular, and everyone seemed to be watching it. The example is a metaphor to help you identify that we live in a world full of Resistance in the form of entertainment. It is exceptionally easy to find things to entertain you. Most of which is going to do nothing for your future.

So, take inspiration from Dr Betty Siegel's story, and make the commitment to become a lifelong learner. It is a simple yet

IDENTIFY STRATEGIES

transformative strategy that can propel you towards the success you desire.

If you have engaged in formal studies, consider setting a standard for your formal education, committing to relevant qualifications and competencies, and cultivating deliberate learning habits. These actions will equip you with the knowledge, skills and experiences necessary to thrive on your path to success.

From a personal perspective, I experienced the power of setting educational standards when I completed my Master of Management program, and four subjects in a Doctor of Business Administration (DBA) program. Despite working full time, raising a young a family and training for marathons, I decided to strive for a High Distinction (HD) average grade for my subjects. Given I achieved this standard for my master's degree, I decided to repeat it for the DBA subjects. One of the subjects was an ungraded pass, and the other three subjects were graded.

To illustrate the power of creative tension, one of the subjects was Quantitative Research Methods. This subject was based on statistics. The last time I had completed a mathematics subject was when I was in the second to last year of high school, where I struggled through a subject called Maths A. My result was a pass with a score of 55%.

Despite my history, I aimed for a HD which meant I had to achieve 80% or better. I'll leave the details to another time, but I achieved 93%, a High Distinction.

Creating standards and doing what you must do to achieve them works. You can make it work for you too.

Please use your notebook and record the strategies you need to action to enable you to move you from your present reality to your vision of life harmony and fulfillment.

Vital Strategy Four: Wealth for Life

Money, as they say, is a means to an end. Understanding the costs associated with your desired future and gaining insights into how money works are essential steps in making wise financial decisions that will propel you towards your goals. What are your mental models about how money works? Is debt okay, or not okay? Is some debt good debt, while other debt is bad debt? Is your focus on growing your income, reducing your expenses or both?

It is important to note that I am not a qualified financial planner or accountant, so I need to be clear that I am not providing direct, personal advice on this matter. It is crucial to consult a professional in this field. The only advice I can offer is broad and not of a specific nature. Seek personal advice from a qualified professional.

If you don't have one, recruit a financial specialist to join your Personal Success Team. This professional can offer valuable insights and guidance tailored to your specific circumstances. As you learn from them, you can begin establishing sound financial management habits. Just as we cultivate learning habits, it is equally important to develop habits that foster financial well-being, based on the knowledge and expertise you gain from the professional you consult.

Embrace the power of knowledge and understanding, symbolised by the word 'and'. The more you educate yourself in this domain and engage in meaningful discussions with experts, the deeper your understanding will become. Challenge the professionals and let them challenge you in return. Expand your knowledge, broaden your perspectives and explore the myriad ways to use your money wisely.

IDENTIFY STRATEGIES

By embracing the power of 'and' you can unlock new possibilities for financial success.

Personally, this is an area where I have had to work hard to learn from experts. This aspect of life did not come natural to me and for long periods of my life, I have made poor decisions. I have trusted people and they have broken that trust. Which has created Resistance to keep learning. Thankfully, I force myself to keep learning and have raised my understanding enough to be able to make better decisions about whom I trust on this topic.

One of the challenges with discussing money and wealth is that it is effectively taboo, and it is one of the last topics people are very open about. It is as if people spoke about it, they would be showing off. Which has made learning about how money works extremely difficult. One of my concerns is that young people who have grown up in the digital age will have no concept of money because all you must do is tap or click to buy something. Tap, tap, tap, click, click, click. I'm not sure that is a useful set of mental models if you want to be able to afford the lifestyle you desire. I am hopeful that young people and families use this book to start being more open about money and wealth creation, and what works and what doesn't work.

Simple strategies for developing good financial habits may include taking control of your credit card usage. Regularly paying interest on your credit card suggests that your current financial practices may benefit from improvement. Similarly, managing your mobile phone or cell phone bill effectively is crucial. If you consistently exceed your plan's limits, it may indicate room for improvement in your financial management.

As mentioned above, another strategy may be to assess your mindset from a financial perspective. What are your mental models about finance and wealth? For example, my parents taught me to save and avoid debt. That was about it. Are those two strategies useful for me? Maybe, maybe not.

It wasn't until I started to educate myself and speak with people who understand money that I began to understand there are a myriad of strategies that I could employ from a wealth creation point of view. Remember, when I say "wealth", I mean you have an economic model that can sustain the life you want to live. The intent of the strategies you identify in this section is to enable you to create the level of wealth necessary to sustain your desired lifestyle.

Topics to consider include:

- Income—how much do you need to fund your desired life?
- Tax—how do you optimise your tax?
- Superannuation (or retirement funds)—how do you optimise this in terms of your overall financial strategy for retirement?
- How do you invest?
- Do investments include the money you spend on developing yourself and growing your business, if you own one?
- What do you purchase that has no true value, but you are using precious money on it?

Being clear about your answers to these questions will help raise the quality of your conversations with your qualified financial expert who can help you create the strategies you need to match your desired lifestyle.

Vital Strategy Five: Career Options

Your ability to exercise choice in your career path grants you freedom, and understanding the defining characteristics of your desired work opens doors to clear options. In your Level One Chart Personal Vision

IDENTIFY STRATEGIES

Summary, you have already identified the qualities and attributes you seek in your ideal work. To address the importance of this vital strategy, I will provide you with an extensive list of suggested strategies tailored to your career journey. Many of you are reading or listening to this book with a primary focus on your career, and I want to ensure you have ample guidance to navigate this realm effectively.

One of the strategies I recommend is actively pursuing opportunities to develop both your technical skills and employability skills. My first book, *What Really Matters For Young Professionals! How to master 15 practices to accelerate your career* is a simple starting point.

Another strategy to consider is documenting stories that highlight your understanding and practical application of employability skills. These stories will serve as powerful evidence of your capabilities.

Furthermore, I encourage you to think beyond traditional work settings when seeking development opportunities. Explore avenues outside your current employment that align with your interests and aspirations. Additionally, engaging a coach or mentor can be immensely beneficial. Personally, I have a set of coaches I have invested in to support me and hold me accountable for my development.

Another avenue for growth is joining relevant LinkedIn groups specific to your industry. If you haven't already, create a LinkedIn profile and learn how to leverage the platform effectively. You can access videos on my YouTube Channel that explain how to effectively use LinkedIn.

Moreover, it is crucial to maintain conscious control over your professional development. You should be the driving force behind your growth and learning. Take deliberate steps to ensure you are actively shaping your development journey and taking ownership of your progress. Never hand the responsibility for your development to your employer, or anyone else for that matter. My *Moving Beyond Being Good* podcast includes numerous interviews with successful people from a variety of industries who demonstrate what taking full responsibility for your development and career looks like. You can also watch these interviews on my podcast playlist on my YouTube Channel.

By implementing these strategies, you can expand your career options and create a pathway towards the fulfilling and rewarding work you desire. Remember, the power to choose lies in your hands.

Far too often, individuals relinquish control of their own development to their organisations. The problem with this approach is that if your organisation fails to invest in your growth, you will not receive the necessary development opportunities. As a result, you become increasingly less employable, a ludicrous strategy to adopt. It is far wiser for you to take charge of your own development.

While it is true that good companies will provide developmental opportunities, it is risky to place 100% of your development in their hands. If they fail to nurture your growth, you will be the one to suffer the consequences. Over time, you become less appealing to your current employer and less attractive to potential future employers. Therefore, it is crucial that you maintain conscious control over your own development.

When we mentioned thinking beyond work for developmental opportunities, consider the value of volunteering. Many individuals volunteer their time and expertise, and there is no need to diminish your contributions by simply labelling yourself as a volunteer. If asked, acknowledge your volunteer work, but also recognise that volunteering often involves high-level responsibilities that parallel paid employment. You should reflect this experience in your resume and confidently discuss it during interviews. If specifically asked about your involvement in volunteering, embrace the opportunity to highlight the valuable skills and knowledge you gained from your experiences.

IDENTIFY STRATEGIES

By retaining conscious control of your development and considering alternative avenues such as volunteering, you will actively shape your professional growth and enhance your employability. Remember, your development is your responsibility, and by taking ownership of it, you can chart a successful and fulfilling career path.

Too often, volunteerism is undervalued by the person doing the volunteer. Their mental model is that because they weren't getting paid for the work, it somehow lost value. This couldn't be further from the truth. When applying for jobs you need not explicitly state that you were a volunteer. Many individuals mistakenly believe that volunteering holds little value in the eyes of employers. However, I can assure you that this perception is flawed. Volunteering offers ample opportunities to develop crucial employability skills. If, for whatever reason, you lack any work experience, it becomes essential for you to gain some through volunteerism if paid employment is not a viable option for you, which can be the circumstance for international students and other non-residents who do not possess a work visa.

To demonstrate to employers that you are not a risk when it comes to collaborating with others, consider immersing yourself in projects or creating your own personal endeavours. Some of the aspirations outlined in your personal plan for success can be shaped into projects. Take on the role of sponsor, project manager and member of the project team; undertake the entire process. Treat it as a project of your own, addressing any issue that arises in your plan. You can explore avenues such as sports, theatre, drama, dance or travel to develop your skills and competencies beyond traditional work settings. The possibilities are vast, and I strongly encourage you to explore these avenues.

By embracing volunteering experiences and engaging in personal projects related to your goals, you will enhance your skill set and expand your competencies. Remember, it is not just about formal work experience; it is about proving your value to employers and showcasing your ability to excel in various contexts. Embrace these opportunities and seize the chance to develop yourself holistically.

Another avenue to consider for career options is to prioritise gaining valuable experience. The harsh reality is that many of you, especially those embarking on your careers early on, simply need to accumulate experience. It's possible that you may enter an organisation with high hopes for its culture, only to realise three months in that it does not align with your expectations.ABRUPTLY quitting and moving on may not be the wisest course of action, as only three months of experience might not carry much weight in your next endeavour. However, if you set a specific time limit, such as eighteen months or two years, for how long you will stay in that culture and concurrently develop a strategy to seek other job opportunities, the combination of these two approaches can prove powerful and effective in helping you transition to an organisation with a culture worthy of your commitment.

As we have seen, there are instances where we engage in strategies that we may not particularly enjoy but pursue them with a clear purpose and focus because we understand how they will lead us to our long-term goals. This deliberate strategy of gaining experience can provide you with greater leverage when it comes to choosing the organisations you wish to work for.

Many of you may aspire to become entrepreneurs. Perhaps you are already on that path or have it planned. By entrepreneurship, I mean running your own business. To navigate this career path, it is crucial to identify the significant questions you have regarding your career. This may involve reflecting on whether your chosen career is the right fit for you or determining if entrepreneurship is truly your desired path. Using the information provided in Chapter 8, create a Level Two Chart outlining the steps you need to take to explore these specific questions. This chart will serve as a guide, outlining the exploration

IDENTIFY STRATEGIES

and research activities necessary for you to delve deeper into your big questions. Furthermore, if your goal is to become an entrepreneur, consider undertaking a mini project focused on understanding the organisational structures required to scale your business.

By gaining relevant experience and exploring your career questions with purpose and focus, you will enhance your career options and pave the way for long-term success.

You may not even be aware of the available opportunities in terms of organisational structures that can support your business. To address this, consider implementing a deliberate strategy by undertaking a mini project to identify the specific organisational structures required for starting and scaling your business over time.

One effective approach could be conducting interviews with successful entrepreneurs. In fact, I currently have a client in my 'Create More Success' program who is conducting informational interviews as part of her research for a career transition. She deliberately seeks out and interviews individuals occupying senior management positions in various industries. This research allows her to gain insights into the actual work being performed and whether it aligns with her own professional experiences. It serves as a deliberate research strategy to guide her decision-making process. These are just a few potential strategies to consider within the career options vital strategy area. Finally, if you are a professional and are considering a career change or a move to a new organisation, I strongly recommend you subscribe to *The Job Hunting* podcast by Renata Bernarde. I have a huge amount of respect for Renata for her dedication and passion for her craft and she is a first-class human being. And yes, you will discover that I am her guest on Episode 128.

Vital Strategy Six: Relationships Matter

It is intrinsic to human nature to yearn for a sense of belonging and to achieve more when collaborating with others. Relationships play a significant role in our success, often more than we realise. As we have explored the concept of a Personal Success Team, it becomes clear that the support and contribution of others are essential for creating your success. Furthermore, it is equally important to assist others in achieving their success.

So, what are some possible strategies to foster meaningful relationships? Taking conscious actions to nurture and support important relationships, as well as mending any strained ones, can be instrumental. If there are any negative aspects present in your current relationships, consider what you can do to transform them into positive ones. Sometimes, a simple apology, even if it wasn't your fault, can serve as a starting point for initiating positive change. Remember, relationships are crucial and require deliberate effort to cultivate and maintain.

If you value someone's presence in your life and desire a positive relationship, sometimes it's necessary to set aside your pride and sincerely apologise, expressing your love for them. I understand it might not be easy, but if the desired outcome is a harmonious relationship, it might be worth considering.

Taking conscious actions to support important relationships also extends to your life partner. Have you both implemented deliberate actions to ensure your love and connection endure? Allow me to share a personal example. My wife and I have five children, yet we make it a point to go on four dedicated dates each year. We treat these occasions as proper dates, dressing up and spending quality time together. This is an intentional strategy for nurturing our relationship.

IDENTIFY STRATEGIES

Similarly, while the children were young, every week, Michelle and I would set aside dedicated 'our time' once the children were in bed. During this period, we engaged in conversation, sat together, or simply enjoyed a movie. It didn't matter which movie we watched; the crucial aspect was intentionally spending time with one another. Today, we walk as much together as possible. We find this allows us to talk about the things that are important on any given day. It's a conscious strategy that we prioritise. Additionally, we plan and pay for our holidays in advance, as mentioned before. Such practices have a positive ripple effect on our relationship. We recognise the benefits of taking vacations and proactively booking and paying for them ahead of time.

Remaining 'in love' requires conscious, dedicated actions. Supporting your partner grow and achieve their desired success is just as important as you growing and achieving your successes.

If you have chosen to become a parent, I encourage to maintain the simple acts of a loving parent that are easier to do when your children are little because children will initiate a lot of the behaviour such as cuddling and telling you they love you. As they get older, the cuddling can become awkward, especially during the teenage years. Nonetheless, find a way to give your children regular hugs. Tell them the things they do that make you proud of them. Have a way of telling them, every day, you love them. My way is, "I luv ya and I miss ya" every time we part.

Identify their unique talents and do what you can to nurture them.

I have wonderful friends who have chosen not to have their own children. The way they support our children and are positive influencers of their lives and do the same for many other children of their close friends is a gift to us all. Parents need the support of great people because as the old saying goes, "It takes a village to raise a child." And these friends know the importance of their role as an 'uncle' or 'aunty', and they consciously choose to cultivate relationships with their 'nieces and nephews' and support them in their lives. This is a conscious, deliberate strategy.

What conscious actions do you undertake to support your important relationships? Creating intentional structures to nurture your key relationships can take various forms, including the examples I've shared. It can also involve simple gestures, like spending ten minutes a day on Facebook, Instagram, WhatsApp, etcetera, engaging with your friends' posts, liking, and leaving comments to let them know you're there and interested in their lives. These small acts can make a significant difference in maintaining and strengthening your relationships.

Making a conscious effort to connect with key people in your life is crucial. Even simple gestures like calling them once a week to say, "Hello, how are you?" or leaving a voicemail message can show that you care and consider them important. These small, deliberate structures allow you to interact with your loved ones and communicate your desire to have them in your life.

Recruiting mentors is a significant aspect to consider. In my extensive research on personal success, I've consistently found that successful individuals actively recruit mentors. They proactively invite these wise individuals into their lives and maintain strong relationships with them. Mentors become integral members of their Personal Success Team, and many people have multiple mentors. So, one deliberate strategy within the 'Relationships Matter' category could be recruiting mentors into your life.

Establishing your Personal Success Team and identifying other individuals whose success teams you can join is another strategy worth pursuing. This approach ensures that you have a network of supportive individuals who contribute to your growth and success. Remember, relationships are reciprocal, and being proactive in nurturing them is essential. Pay attention to what's happening in other people's lives and remember that even the little things matter. Incorporate these considerations into your strategies to help manifest the success you desire.

IDENTIFY STRATEGIES

Six Vital Strategies Summary

Once you have developed at least one strategy for each of the six vital strategy areas, it's crucial to review them. When evaluating each strategy, consider whether it will truly help you progress from your current position to where you want to be. It's up to you to determine if the strategy is useful and relevant based on your present reality and your personal vision summary. Will it contribute to moving you at least part of the way in the desired direction? Assess whether the strategies you've chosen collectively align with your vision. Use a highlighter to identify the vital strategies that seem like they will have the most impact on your vision.

It's important to recognise that when you review all your strategies, you might find that they don't take you all the way to your desired outcome. Depending on the timeframe outlined in your personal vision summary, these strategies may only cover the next three to twelve months or possibly up to twenty-four months. This is perfectly normal and acceptable. Remember, you can always reinvigorate and update your strategies as you progress along your journey.

Take a moment to reflect on your vision and present reality. Are there any gaps between the two? If you identify any gaps, consider whether they correspond to a specific vital strategy area. In such cases, you can add relevant strategies to address those gaps and further propel you towards your desired destination. Continually adapting and adding strategies is a natural part of the process, ensuring that you effectively bridge the gap between where you currently stand and where you aspire to be.

It's important to assess the ease of each step in your strategies. Identify the ones that are like low-hanging fruit, the ones that you can easily tackle and get moving on. Also, consider which ones may be more challenging but have the potential to yield the most significant results. Which strategies will have a domino effect on the other strategies? These are your high leverage strategies. When determining if they are doable, your mental models play a crucial role. Your mental models will influence your perception of whether these steps are achievable or not. Many things are more doable than you may initially realise. Taking that first step and getting started is often the key. Additionally, enlisting the support of others in your Personal Success Team can help hold you accountable and ensure that your strategies remain doable. So, ask yourself, are they truly doable?

Now, here's something vital to understand: Sometimes, to achieve your major goals, you must adopt strategies that you don't particularly enjoy. For instance, when I was publishing my first book, I had to put in long hours of writing and editing, meticulously reviewing the feedback I received. It wasn't always pleasant, staying up late and doing that work. However, I recognised that to meet my publishing deadline and fulfill my vision, it was necessary. I didn't want to give up on my vision, so I pushed through the smart, hard work.

When I wrote the next two books, including this one, I knew what I was going to have to do, but I also knew the feeling you get from successfully publishing a book, so my vision was more vivid. While the smart, hard work of writing was still required, somehow it was 'easier' because I knew the value of it.

These examples illustrate that there are tasks we may not enjoy, yet we recognise their importance in helping us achieve the success we desire. It's about recognising the necessity of completing these tasks and being willing to put in the hard work, even when it's not our preference.

Now that we have completed identifying strategies for your Level One Chart, most, if not all, of your strategies will consist of concise single sentences. However, the challenge lies in the fact that many of these strategies don't provide you with precise instructions on what needs to be done. They offer direction and focus, but they lack the necessary specificity.

IDENTIFY STRATEGIES

To address this, we need to create the Level Two Charts. We must delve deeper into each strategy in your Level One Chart and expand on them to gain clarity. We need to 'double click' on each strategy and examine the specific strategic outcome we desire. What are the specific details regarding the present reality that pertain to that strategy? Then, it's time to engage in a brainstorming process to generate a list of actions. This will allow you to become clear about the specific steps you need to take to bring your vision to life. It's like elastic bands within elastic bands, using that metaphor to illustrate the interconnected nature of the process.

As we conclude this chapter, let's turn our attention to what lies ahead. Chapter 8 awaits us: Level Two Charts. In this next chapter, I will guide you through the process and equip you with the necessary tools to transform the strategies you've identified in your Level One Chart into Level Two Charts. These Level Two Charts will provide you with precise instructions on what actions you need to take to create the success you desire.

CHAPTER 8

LEVEL TWO CHARTS

"Devil's in the detail, but so is salvation."

Hyman G. Rickover

In this chapter, I will demonstrate just how simple it is to develop your Level Two Charts for each vital strategy outlined in your Level One Chart for life harmony and personal success.

Please have your notebook ready. For each Level Two Chart, divide your page into three sections. At the top of the page, name the Vital Strategy category from which the Level Two Chart strategy is going to be created. Next name the strategy. You can see in the example in Figure 8 Level Two Chart example, the Vital Strategy category is Self-Awareness, and the strategy, 'Create my Personal Success Team'.

You will see the top section is Step One, where you will clarify what success looks like for the specific Vital Strategy from your Level One Chart, the middle section will be where you will write your actions for that strategy, which is Step Three in this process, and the bottom section is where you will write your present reality as it relates to the specific vital strategy you are focusing on.

LEVEL TWO CHARTS

Setting your page up like this is like the elastic band metaphor; the top of the page represents the top of the elastic band, the bottom of the page is the bottom of the elastic band, and the middle of the page is the middle of the elastic that is being stretched and provides you with the energy for action.

Figure 7 Elastic Band Metaphor

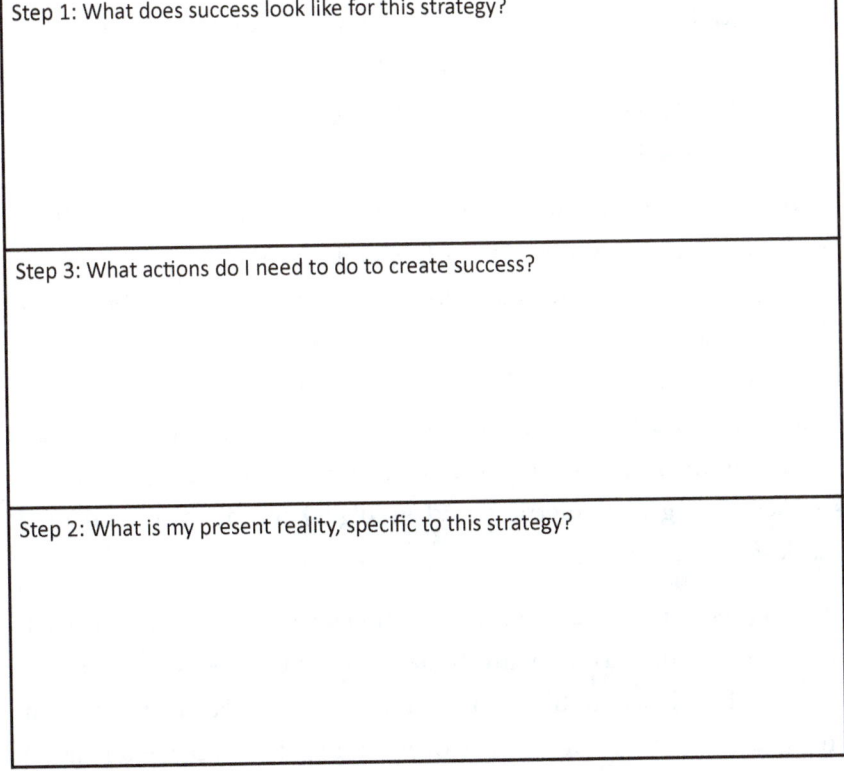

Figure 8 Level Two Chart Example

Viral Strategy: Self Awareness
Strategy: Create my Personal Success Team

Step 1: What does success look like for this strategy?
Step 3: What actions do I need to do to create success?
Step 2: What is my present reality, specific to this strategy?

If you have become a member of the Yes For Success Online Course, all these resources are available to you, as it is in the exclusive Facebook Group where you can ask questions, see examples from others, and have access to live sessions to further develop your understanding and implementation of your strategies.

As an example, you may have a vital strategy in your Fitness and Health section that says something like, "Lose 10 kg."

As you commence your Level Two Chart, the first step is to be specific about the desired outcome you want to achieve. In the top section of your chart, take the one-line title from your Level One Chart and dive deeper into what it truly means. "Lose 10 kg" may seem sufficient, but it's important to provide more detail. Let me share a real example from my personal experience over time. My outcome for the support chart titled "Weigh 83 kg plus or minus 2 kg" included the following: "I want to feel better about myself, have more energy, reduce and eliminate heartburn associated with being overweight, and maintain a weight goal on an ongoing basis."

Next, let's focus on your starting point. In my case, I weighed 90 kg and noticed that my clothes no longer fit as they used to. Despite being physically active with activities like running, walking, biking and coaching junior sports, there were other aspects of my present reality that weren't great. I realised I was consuming fast food too regularly, experiencing heartburn daily (with a possible link to bread), and had genetically high cholesterol. Additionally, I had the habit of eating a second serving at dinnertime and indulging in chocolate and other snacks after dinner.

Steps Three and Four involve determining what actions you will take to move from your starting point to the desired outcome for this specific strategy. This is where brainstorming comes into play. Here are some steps I came up with for my own journey: trial giving up bread to assess its impact on heartburn; visit a doctor if heartburn persists; have fruit for breakfast; include more canned tuna in my lunch; limit dinner to a single serving; eliminate after-dinner snacks; embrace the feeling of hunger and shift my mindset to view it as a positive sensation; cut out soft drinks and only consume water or sparkling water with meals; continue exercising at my current level; and start a weekly weigh-in routine (which I had previously neglected). It was important for me to realise that despite my exercise routine, I needed to address my calorie intake and make healthier choices.

By following these steps, you can gain clarity on the actions required to bridge the gap between your starting point and the desired outcome for each specific strategy.

You are now at the fourth step in the process. Step Four involves determining the order in which you will take these actions. In my case, I highlighted all the actions on my Level Two Chart that I would begin immediately, which were:

- Trial giving up bread to assess its impact on heartburn.
- Have fruit for breakfast.
- Include more canned tuna in my lunch.
- Limit dinner to a single serving
- Eliminate after-dinner snacks.
- Embrace the feeling of hunger and shift my mindset to view it as a positive sensation.
- Cut out soft drinks and only consume water or sparkling water with meals.
- Continue exercising at my current level.
- Start a weekly weigh-in routine and report my weight to a friend.

Additionally, I made a note that if my heartburn didn't reduce within three weeks, I would schedule a visit to the doctor. This provided some structure to the brainstorming process. Although not explicitly mentioned, I gave myself three months to assess the effectiveness of these actions.

As you can see, the Level Two Chart outlined exactly what I needed to do. I can personally attest to the empowerment it brings. Within just four weeks, I had already lost 5.2 kg. It truly worked.

Occasionally, you will need to go to another level of detail, which is when you use a Level Three Chart.

Level Three Charts

Let's dive into an example to illustrate the process. In 2007, one of my vital strategies was to establish a successful business. To define this vision for my career, I compiled a comprehensive Level Two Chart list outlining what constituted a successful business. This information was completed at the top of the chart. It included details regarding revenue, happy customers, the type of customers I would be serving and more. I noted the pertinent details on the bottom of the chart that reflected my present reality as it related to starting my own successful business. This included my corporate experience and acknowledged that while I had been involved in starting a new corporate entity, I had never launched my own business before. The middle section of the chart included all the actions I was going to need to do to create my business, one of which was to become an author.

Given I had never embarked on that endeavour before, I took it a step further by delving into a Level Three Chart. This chart enabled me to become clearer about what success for the book looked like, as well as assessing my present reality as it specifically related to writing. My actions included researching a book writing course and recruiting a specific mentor for book writing into my Personal Success Team. While it may seem like it takes forever to complete these charts, this chart literally took less than ten minutes. This smart, hard work saved me weeks, if not months of time and provided me with clarity about the steps I needed to take to create the future I desired.

It is important to note that for most of the actions you identify in your Level Two Charts, you won't need to create a Level Three Chart. Most of the detail for your plan will be finalised in your Level Two Charts, with only a few exceptions requiring the additional detail a Level Three Chart provides, such as the example with writing my first book.

Level Three Chart Book example

Level Two Chart Action: Write a book.

Please remember that the example follows the metaphor of the stretched elastic band. Step One represents the top of the elastic band, Step Two represents the bottom of the elastic band, and Step Three represents the middle of the elastic band where the potential energy with the elastic band 'stretched' creates the kinetic energy for action to create the outcome your desire. This is why Step Three is listed in between Steps One and Two.

Step One: What does success look like for this strategy?

- Sell at least three thousand books in physical and eBook formats.
- Package the book with development programs for both corporate and university development programs.
- Create an online course that supports and supplements the book's contents.
- The book will be up to one hundred and fifty pages for ease of consumption for the target audience who are early career

starters or university students in the last two years of their course.

- Publish the book by July 2010.

Step Three: What actions do I need to do to create success?

- Recruit a mentor into my Personal Success Team who can guide me with my writing (this action requires research).
    - o The following actions were added after I recruited my mentor:
        - Create a free blog.
        - Start posting articles.
        - Send articles to people for feedback.
        - Review which articles seem to 'connect' the most with my audience.
        - When errors are detected, edit the article, and correct the errors and republish the article.
- Complete a book writing a publishing course (this action requires research).
- Name the book, *What Really Matters for Young Professionals! How to Master 15 Practices to Accelerate Your Career.*
- Create an 'order' and flow for the book.
- Complete the book writing and publishing process.

Step Two: What is my present reality specific to this strategy?

- I have never published a book.
- I was one of six contributing authors to an academic paper published in an academic journal.
- I don't know if I am good at writing.

LEVEL TWO CHARTS

- I occasionally write reports for my job and haven't received feedback criticising my writing style, but I haven't received any feedback praising it either.
- I do have a clear idea about what I want to write about and who the target audience is.

Use your notebook to complete any required Level Three Charts.

The next step is the creation of your ninety-day plan.

Creating a Ninety-Day Plan

This is an exciting juncture where we'll help you channel your focus towards the next ninety days, a period that can catalyse transformative changes in your life. Over the years, I've witnessed the magic that unfolds when individuals commit to ninety-day plans. Not only does it sharpen your focus, but it also harnesses the intrinsic motivation that propels you towards the success you crave.

Now, let's get started on your transformative journey. To fully grasp the wisdom in this chapter, you'll need to have your ninety-day plan template and personal vision summary at your fingertips. Please visit https://orgsthatmatter.com/yfsresources to download your ninety-day plan template. Also, ensure access to all those invaluable Level Two Charts you've diligently crafted. I know it may seem like a lot, but it's all part of the process, and it's going to make sense as we proceed.

By now, you've successfully completed your Level One Chart and numerous Level Two Charts, and possibly even ventured into some Level Three Charts. If you have Level Three Charts, kudos to your dedication. Please have those handy as well. Your workspace may seem cluttered, but remember, we're orchestrating all this information to craft your ninety-day plan efficiently.

Your goal with this ninety-day plan is to provide you with an unwavering focus on every facet of your life. I aim to steer you towards the life you desire while enhancing your awareness of what truly makes you happy along the way. This journey is a self-reinforcing loop—as you see progress and feel good about your actions, your awareness will soar.

Now, let's dive into the steps for creating your ninety-day plan:

Step One: Copy your personal vision summary from your Level One Chart. Highlight it and make a copy. Having it in an electronic format simplifies this step. Paste it into the designated section of your ninety-day plan. You have two pages for this purpose, and if you need more space, don't hesitate to expand it. Your personal vision summary is your North Star, guiding every action you take over the next ninety days.

Step Two: Review all your Level Two and Level Three Charts. Take a moment to go through all the actions you've outlined in these charts. Highlight the ones that you believe should be tackled within the next ninety days. At this stage, it's common to find numerous actions for your first ninety days—don't fret about it. We'll address that later in Chapter 10. Focus on each chart individually, identifying which actions need immediate attention.

Step Three: Copy all the highlighted actions from Step Two and paste them into the relevant sections of your ninety-day plan. Categorise them according to your vital strategies, aligning each action with the

LEVEL TWO CHARTS

appropriate section. This step will help you visualise the balance you're creating for yourself over the next ninety days.

Remember, it's normal for some vital strategies to receive more attention in this plan than others. What matters most is ensuring that you commit to at least one action in each of the six vital strategies during this ninety-day period, maintaining a sense of balance as you define it for yourself.

Once your ninety-day plan is populated with these actions, it's ready to guide you through the next three months. As you complete each action, mark it as done. The inclusion of your personal vision summary ensures that every action you take is linked to your bigger picture. This connection is what empowers you to make the right choices and understand the cost of inaction.

Now, let's delve deeper into the nuances of crafting your ninety-day plan and address some common concerns:

Step Four: As you proceed, consider the power of visualisation. Your personal vision summary might span five, ten or even twenty years into the future. This grand vision is what fuels your motivation and connects your daily actions to the bigger picture. Whenever you're faced with a choice to act or not, you'll clearly see the consequences, reinforcing your commitment to your vision.

Step Five: Rejoice in the fact that you now possess a complete ninety-day plan. This is a pivotal moment on your journey to personal growth and fulfillment. It's not just about checking off tasks; it's about a holistic transformation that will reverberate through your life.

In essence, you have engaged in a process of copying and pasting, yet the results are nothing short of transformative. The moment you complete this plan is a milestone worth celebrating. I'm thrilled to imagine you, wherever you are, with a completed plan and unwavering focus for the next ninety days.

Now, you might have concerns about the volume of actions or potential overwhelm. Rest assured; we'll address these concerns in Chapters 9 and 10. For now, trust your intuition as you populate your plan. If it's your first time, understand that your plan may not be perfect, and that's perfectly fine. It's a journey, and your tenth plan will be even better.

I can't emphasise enough how exhilarating it is to have a roadmap that guides your actions and a laser-sharp focus for the next ninety days. Embrace this moment, and don't be discouraged if your plan seems ambitious.

Remember this is a journey towards life harmony, fulfillment and success. You're not alone in this endeavour. Alongside you, there are others who are seeking the same path, including parents who want to positively influence their children and individuals who want to inspire those around them. If you are concerned about staying the course, this is the power of the Yes For Success Online Course and the community that exists to support each other as you execute your plan.

As you embark on this ninety-day journey, stay open to the transformative power it holds. Trust the process. Each action you take brings you one step closer to the life you desire. Notice your progress because progress matters!

In Chapters 9 and 10, we'll explore how to manage your plan effectively, whether you've packed it to the brim or find yourself adjusting as you go. Until then, celebrate your achievements and brace yourself for the incredible transformation that awaits.

Now, let's get started on putting your ninety-day plan into action, which takes us to Chapter 9: Perform.

CHAPTER 9

PERFORM

"Action is the foundational key to all success."

Pablo Picasso

This is an exhilarating phase where we act and breathe life into your plan.

Ultimately, nothing comes to fruition without acting. Your plans hold no weight if you don't put them into practice. If you genuinely seek the success you've outlined in your plan, then you must take action. This chapter is all about taking decisive steps forward.

Please use your notebook and answer this question, "What will achieving your plan and bringing it to life be worth to you?"

Some people express their answer using numbers, often resulting in substantial figures. Others choose to convey the significance of creating the success they desire using descriptive terms like 'priceless' or 'invaluable'. Whatever your answer is, I urge you to identify precisely what it would be worth to you.

Never forget the profound meaning your plan holds for you and the immense value it carries. Remind yourself of what it truly means to actualise this plan.

Now that you have a fully developed plan and a clear understanding of its worth to you, it's crucial to place your plan, ideally your ninety-day plan or at the very least your Personal Vision Summary, in a location where you can encounter it regularly. Literally affix it to a wall where you can see it daily. This serves as a constant reminder. People often stick it on the back of their door, in their bathroom or in their study. Some even place it in multiple spots. The important thing is to position it where you will frequently encounter it, ensuring that you never forget two essential aspects: a) what you aspire to create in your life, and b) what it truly means to you.

For those who possess a more visual inclination and appreciate imagery, creating a vision board might be an appealing option. But what exactly is a vision board? Essentially, it is a board adorned with an array of pictures that symbolise the elements encompassed within your vision. These pictures need not be exact representations; they simply serve as symbolic depictions aligned with your personal vision summary.

For instance, you might include pictures of destinations you aspire to visit. Or perhaps images of a key, which may represent a home, a car or a holiday getaway, depending on your individual interpretation. The key acts as a symbolic representation for you. You might also incorporate images that portray the quality of relationships you desire. For instance, a picture featuring two children walking hand in hand on a beach, symbolising a close bond, can represent the significance of key relationships highlighted in your personal vision summary.

It could be a simple act of leaping for joy and exuding passion. If passion is a significant element in your personal vision summary, then you'll want to include an image or illustration that embodies passion

PERFORM

for you. It could be a depiction of someone joyfully leaping at sunset on a beach. The specific images you choose are not as important as the personal meaning they hold for you and how they represent the elements you have written in your personal vision summary.

For some of you, family may be a crucial component of your Personal Vision Summary. Even if you don't currently have a family or a partner, you might include a photo that symbolises your desired family life on your vision board. This serves as a reminder of what you aspire to create in terms of personal success.

You may also include images related to hobbies, activities, passions or any pursuits you aspire to engage in. These images can even feature yourself participating in those activities currently, as your vision can incorporate aspects of your present reality that you wish to carry forward into your future.

If your vision revolves around your career, you could include an image depicting a role you desire or the type of career you aspire to have. Choose an image that resonates with you and represents the career path you envision. By incorporating these diverse elements onto your vision board, you create a visual and pictorial representation that aligns with the words you have penned in your personal vision summary.

For many individuals, a vision board proves to be a powerful tool in maintaining focus and serving as a daily reminder of the elements encompassed within their personal vision summary. It reinforces the worth of their vision and emphasises the importance of taking action to bring it to life.

Another effective way to support your progress in the 'Perform' stage is by sharing your plan with someone you trust. It can be immensely helpful to confide in a trusted individual and disclose your plan to them. If you have a life partner who is an integral part of your envisioned success, I strongly recommend sharing your plan with them. Share as much as you feel comfortable and ask them to hold you accountable. Request their support in regularly checking in on your progress, celebrating your achievements and providing motivation. You require both intrinsic and external motivation, as well as recognition, to propel you forward on your journey. Therefore, I encourage you to confide in someone you trust, preferably someone who is likely to be a valuable member of your Personal Success Team.

However, it's important to remember that your plan holds no meaning if you fail to take action. I've already emphasised this, and I'll reiterate it once again: your plan remains inconsequential if you don't follow through with the actions outlined within it. Taking action is crucial. It's likely that you'll need to continuously assess and adjust your mindset when it comes to taking action.

Your mindset, particularly concerning action-taking, can often hinder your progress towards the desired success. You will need to confront and challenge the barriers you've set for yourself; barriers that dictate what you believe you can or cannot accomplish. In my own business journey, I had held a belief for quite some time that marketing was an unethical endeavour and that marketers were solely focused on extracting money from people for their good, and not the good of customers. However, if I truly wanted to achieve greater success in my business, I had to shift my mindset regarding marketing. I had to let go of those limiting beliefs and embrace a new perspective. If I believed in my products and services and that they enhance people's lives, then I must market those products and services otherwise, who would know they exist? And if people don't know they exist, how can they benefit from them? I had to make that mindset shift. In fact, I now believe I have a duty to market what I do because I believe in it so much!

Remember, acting and continuously examining and transforming your mindset are essential components on the path to creating the success you desire.

You will face similar challenges along your journey, but it's crucial that you confront them and be willing to break free from the chains of your mental models. We touched upon this topic in Chapter 2 when discussing mental models and Resistance, and it carries through to acting. Resistance is your enemy. It will have a strong presence now you have created your plan. Defeat it, every day!

Another quote by Dewitt Jones I support is, "Hey, it's not trespassing to go beyond your own boundaries." And it truly isn't. You must be prepared to break free from the limitations of your mental models and venture beyond your self-imposed boundaries to take the necessary actions to bring your plans to life.

Developing rituals is essential; rituals encompass the habits and regular behaviours you engage in. Let me share an example of one of my rituals for times when things don't go as planned. I turn to my 'grateful list'. It's a list I keep on the wall of my office, right next to my computer screen. Whenever things veer off track—because, let's face it, that can happen as we progress on our plan's journey—I immediately look at my 'grateful list'. I scan through each and every item, reminding myself of all the things I'm grateful for. Instantly, a sense of gratitude washes over me, and it's remarkable how the issue that was troubling me no longer seems as significant. I realise the abundance of things I already possess and appreciate in my life, which puts me in a better mindset to tackle whatever problem or challenge arises at any given moment.

I also have a ritual to ask myself the following question when things don't go as I had expected. I ask myself, "Okay, Gazza, what's the opportunity here?"

You may recall I did this when my business was impacted by the start of pandemic when 90% of my business was stopped or 'paused'. The outcome of asking myself, "What is the opportunity here?" was the creation of my #1 Amazon Kindle Bestseller *Disruption Leadership*

YES FOR SUCCESS

Matters: lessons for leaders from the pandemic which became a catalyst to restoring and growing my business over the ensuing years.

Remember, breaking free from the chains of your mindset, embracing new perspectives and cultivating rituals are powerful tools that support you in creating the success you desire.

So even something as simple as maintaining a 'grateful list', or training yourself to ask, "What's the opportunity here?" can become a ritual. Likewise, having a vision board and intentionally looking at it once a day can be a ritual. Reviewing your big goals using the notes function in your phone and recording an example of magic that occurred during the day are rituals that can influence your mind in a positive way while you are asleep, enabling you to wake up the next day excited and energised for what the new day will bring.

Recognising your progress and celebrating your achievements along the way is also a ritual. In Chapter 3 I mentioned the importance of having a vision to 'pull' you forward towards happiness, life harmony and success, so you must recognise the 'moments' along your journey that provide happiness now. If happiness is all in 'the future' you will never be happy. Become a master at this recommended ritual. Stop. Reflect. Notice your successes. Celebrate them!

The way you start your mornings, the rituals you establish around breakfast, exercise, and even your work and personal development activities, all these can become powerful rituals that support your journey towards success.

You may wonder, "Gary, what if I stumble? What if I faithfully follow these rituals, challenge my mental models, break free from its chains, regularly defeat Resistance, but then suddenly, I fall off the horse? What do I do then? Does that mean the rituals were futile? Does it imply that what I planned doesn't work anymore?"

PERFORM

Well, let me assure you that stumbling along the way is a natural part of the process. It doesn't diminish the value of the rituals you've embraced or the plan you've crafted. In fact, it is in those moments of stumbling and encountering setbacks that the true power of your rituals and your plan becomes apparent. These challenging moments offer opportunities for growth, learning and resilience.

When you fall off the horse, take a moment to reflect and assess what happened. Was it a temporary setback, or does it require a shift in your approach? Use this as an opportunity to refine your rituals and re-evaluate your plan. Sometimes, unexpected detours lead you to even greater achievements and insights you wouldn't have gained otherwise.

Remember, success is not defined by a smooth, uninterrupted journey. It's about your ability to adapt, persevere and keep moving forward. So, even when you stumble, don't lose sight of your vision, your rituals or the worth of your plan. Embrace the challenges as opportunities for growth, and trust that your commitment to taking action will ultimately lead you to the success you desire. Use the successes you have achieved along the journey as evidence that you can focus and do the smart, hard work to achieve success, because you have already done it, time and again.

We all have moments when we fall off the horse, me included. I know firsthand that during periods of intense travel for work, my rituals face significant strain and stress, especially when it comes to maintaining a consistent eating routine. It becomes more challenging to manage my food choices, and there are times when my diet veers off track. It can happen subtly, without even realising it.

One day, it hits you like a hard fall when you come off a horse. Sometimes, that fall can last for quite a while, as if it happened in mega slow motion because it takes days, weeks, gosh, sometime months before you realise you've fallen, and then suddenly, you hit the ground and think, "Oh my, I recognise what's happened. I've fallen off the horse. Bam! Wow, all right, what do I do now?"

The answer is simple. Once you recognise that you've fallen off the horse and that the rituals you've been practising successfully for a long time have somehow stopped, you must understand that it wasn't the rituals that failed; it was you who stopped doing them. So, what do you do?

You just get back on the horse.

Yes, you heard me right. You just get back on the horse.

There's no need to whip or punish yourself. Dust yourself off, climb back on that horse and keep going. Keep embracing your rituals as they are the key to creating the success you envision in your plan. It's natural to fall off the horse from time to time. When you realise you've strayed, simply get back on track.

It's important to recognise that blaming the rituals instead of taking responsibility for your actions only leads to further entrapment within limiting mindsets. That's when everything grinds to a halt. So, as you hold on to your plan and continue with your rituals, remember that during the review phase, which we'll discuss in Chapter 10, you'll have the opportunity to assess your progress and ensure you're on the right path. Stay committed to your rituals and follow the roadmap outlined in your plan. And if you happen to recognise that you've fallen off the horse, just get back on as there is no need to stress about it. Move forward, take action and leave the worries behind. There's no point in dwelling on what's already happened, get back on the horse and keep going.

Let's recap your journey through this book. You have explored the concept of the elastic band of life and how it operates on multiple levels. This fundamental structure provides the energy and focus necessary to create your future. You have delved into extensive background research and focused on vital principles for personal success: passion, personal vision, present reality, prioritising strategies and performance. You also identified vital strategies within six categories, understanding that it's essential to engage in at least one action within each strategy throughout your ninety-day plan to create your desired success. These strategies include self-awareness, fitness and health, learn for success, wealth for life, career options and relationships matter. You now have completed your plan to guide you in creating your unique version of life harmony, success and fulfillment. Congratulations!

The final topic to explore is the review process. Now, it is time to move to Chapter 10: Review.

CHAPTER 10

REVIEW

"It is not the strongest of the species that survive, nor the most intelligent, but the one most responsive to change."

Charles Darwin

I strongly encourage you to update your ninety-day plan regularly, ideally every ninety days (yes, that makes sense, doesn't it!). It may sound peculiar, but as they say, even at Disneyland in Anaheim, USA, the most frequently asked question is, "What time is the 3 p.m. parade?"

Sometimes, it's necessary to be explicit to ensure clarity ☺!

Updating your ninety-day plan every ninety days means you'll go through four cycles each year. The primary focus of this plan is to assess your progress. In your first plan, it's natural to make your best guess regarding what you can accomplish within those initial ninety days. You'll be amazed at how much you can actually achieve in that timeframe, but it's possible that some tasks may remain incomplete. Remember, it's not the end of the world. Keep your focus on the fact that you've made progress. Celebrate progress. Notice it. See it. Let it inject confidence into your future actions.

Recognise Resistance when it raises its ugly head and says, "You have done enough! This stuff doesn't work!"

It does work and your progress is all the evidence you need!

REVIEW

As you progress, you'll find that your planning skills improve significantly. One challenge we face as adults is expecting immediate mastery when learning something new. We often place pressure on ourselves to achieve an 8, 9, or 10 out of 10, right from the start. However, life has taught us that acquiring new skills takes time and patience, and planning for personal success is no exception. Remember, you're developing this skill, and by the time you reach your third and fourth cycles, you'll be amazed at how much you've improved and how deeply you understand the process.

Persistence is key. Don't be disheartened if you discover that you haven't completed everything you initially wrote down in your first ninety-day plan. Take note of how far you've come and recognise that you've made substantial progress. It's important to acknowledge that you're moving in the direction you desired, overcoming the obstacles of procrastination and perfectionism. You're learning to live with them while still making progress happen.

For the items that remain on your list, it's crucial to reflect on why they weren't completed. It could be a matter of not having enough time or having overloaded your initial list. However, it's essential to be brutally honest with yourself. Were you avoiding those tasks, or did you genuinely have too much on your plate? Take the time to assess and understand the reasons behind their incomplete status.

It's important to evaluate the relevance of the actions you've identified. Throughout this process, you may realise that certain tasks you initially thought were necessary won't help you create the future you desire. In such cases, you must stop doing them or discard them altogether. Ask yourself: Are the actions I planned still relevant? If they are, copy and paste them into your new ninety-day plan. Remind yourself of your Personal Vision Summary and refer to your Level Two Charts to determine which actions from there need to be included in your updated plan. If necessary, update your Level Two Charts as well.

Keep in mind that many Level Two Charts may span longer periods than three months, but if they don't, you may need to revise them as well.

Regularly review your Personal Vision Summary. I recommend doing this every six to twelve months, although the timeframe may vary for each person. When updating your ninety-day plans, you'll primarily focus on the immediate ninety-day level, as the overall vision doesn't typically change. However, taking the time to review your entire plan, starting from the Personal Vision Summary, at least once a year, and sometimes twice, can be beneficial. As you progress through this process, you'll gain clarity about what you truly want, and your Personal Vision Summary may evolve accordingly.

Over time, as you review and refine your ninety-day plans, you may find subtle enhancements to your Personal Vision Summary. Embrace these improvements; they contribute to the ongoing refinement of your vision. Remember, your plan is a living document that can adapt and grow with you. You can expect these refinements to occur through the first year of creating the life you desire, as you become clearer about what you really want in life. This is 100% okay and normal.

If you wish to conduct a comprehensive review of your plan, you can simply revisit Chapters 4 to 8 and create new documents accordingly.

What if you encounter roadblocks in your journey, such as illness, loss, job termination or economic crises? Life is filled with unexpected challenges and roadblocks; they can and do happen. Even the most meticulously crafted plans can be tested when faced with these obstacles. The key for you is to acknowledge that roadblocks are a part of life and accept their presence.

So, how do you deal with roadblocks when they arise? Firstly, understand that the world operates in curves rather than straight lines.

I've personally experienced roadblocks in my own life and have shared numerous examples throughout this book.

Roadblocks can be catalysts for transformation. They force us to confront ourselves and learn invaluable lessons amidst the adversity. Although the experience may be arduous, it opens doors to personal growth and resilience. It is through navigating the hardships that we can shape our future and embrace the opportunities that lie ahead.

Over time, I've developed a model to help us navigate this reality. During the turning-points activities you completed in Chapter 2, individuals often come to realise that life can throw tough challenges your way. Unexpected events can occur, seemingly out of the blue. When faced with such situations, it's crucial to acknowledge the harsh reality they present. Whether you've recently lost your job, experienced the end of a relationship or encountered a tragic event like the passing of a loved one, you must embrace the brutal truth of these circumstances.

Allow yourself to go through the necessary mourning process and seek support during this time. It's perfectly okay to lean on others for assistance and your Personal Success Team becomes a vital support during these periods. However, even during your grieving, never lose sight of the belief that, at some point in the future, though the exact duration may remain uncertain, you will emerge stronger from this experience. While you had no control over the event itself, you have the power to shape how you interpret it and how you use it as a valuable learning opportunity to propel yourself forward. It took me several years to make sense of the car accident I was involved in, but eventually, I learned to grow as a person from that challenging experience. I would not have authored this book if that horrible experience had not occurred.

It was through another significant event, my father's battle with cancer and my role in caring for him at home, that I came to a profound realisation. During the process of nursing him, I discovered an inner strength and resilience within myself. It was as if that deep understanding and knowledge had a profound awakening within me. I realised that, astonishingly, I had somehow become a better person because of the terrible experience of the car accident.

Life's trials have a way of revealing our hidden capacities and fostering personal growth. While we may not comprehend the purpose or meaning behind difficult circumstances immediately, with time, we can begin to see how they shape us into stronger individuals.

It's the yin and yang model: accepting the brutal reality when roadblocks arise, while never losing faith that, in due course, you will reflect and feel a sense of gratitude for the experience, the lessons learned and the person you have become as a result. I appreciate this is hard when you are in the thick of a difficult time. Have faith, you will grow from it. After all, you can't change what has happened, can you?

During such times, it's essential to lean on the members of your Personal Success Team to support you because the duration of gaining clarity may be uncertain. Significant emotional events have the potential to reshape your entire vision, and that's perfectly fine. Clarity can unexpectedly emerge, even when you thought you had it all figured out. When faced with a roadblock, it can be like a sudden awakening that brings newfound clarity, prompting you to re-evaluate and revise your plan.

As you navigate this journey, there will be points where roadblocks appear, and you may find yourself in need of pausing or slowing down. While it's crucial to maintain rituals that contribute to your progress as much as possible, I understand that significant life events can leave you needing rest, periods where sleep becomes paramount, allowing your body, spirit and mental health to recover. And although you may not be

REVIEW

able to sustain all your rituals during this time, strive to maintain those you can manage and tolerate.

A moment will come when you feel ready to begin anew. It might entail starting from scratch, returning to Chapter 1, and working your way back through the chapters to create a fresh plan. Alternatively, it could reaffirm the existing plan, but now you're in a mental, physical and spiritual space where you can mount the horse and set off again. You will recognise this readiness within yourself, and if you have been relying on the support of your Personal Success Team, they will also guide you in discerning when it's time to get back on the horse and continue moving forward. The timeframe for this varies from person to person, and speaking from personal experience, I cannot provide an exact duration.

Another strategy during difficult times is to ask, "Who can I help?" Shifting your focus to helping someone for whom you may be a member of their Personal Success Team is a powerful strategy in that it provides purpose and clarity in an otherwise cluttered period.

Executing your plan is worth it. You will have noticed benefits and successes occurring throughout the development of your plan. You will have started new habits and rituals that have already paid off with small 'wins', possibly even big ones! With a clear direction you are in control of your choices, time and energy. It creates the sense of harmony 'today' that enhances the probability of you creating it again tomorrow, and the next day and so on.

With that, I express my gratitude. Thank you for completing the ten chapters of this book. However, this is not the end of the journey; it is merely the beginning.

With all the Resistance present in the world, I encourage to join the *Yes For Success* Online Course to gain access to like-minded people who are supporting, encouraging and celebrating each other achieving life harmony and fulfillment. I extend my heartfelt thanks to you for purchasing this book and more importantly, for investing in yourself. Your future is worth it!

CHAPTER 11

YES FOR SUCCESS CORPORATE PROGRAM

"Success isn't just about what you achieve at work; it's also about the dreams your employees fulfill beyond the office walls. Embrace their personal victories, and watch your company thrive."

Gary Ryan

Imagine if the staff in your organisation completed the *Yes For Success* program and then shared and celebrated their life achievements over time. Examples would include a staff member completing a 5-kilometre walk. Another reaches and maintains a healthy weight goal. Another purchases their first investment property. Another experiences a European trip of a lifetime, another treks to the top of Mt Kilimanjaro. Yet another buys their dream car. Another raises $10,000 for a charity. Another travels to Cambodia and serves on a project for a month building a freshwater pipeline for a remote village. Another finds their dream partner and asks them to marry them. Another plays bass guitar in a band in front of a live audience. Another is the star in an amateur theatre play. Another sends their child to a school they once believed was out of reach. Another starts playing indoor mixed netball, the first time they have played a team sport in their life, and they win the pennant. Another completes a formal qualification they had once believed was impossible. Another passes their test to fly a solo plane. Another records a song. Another changes their career. Another doubles their income. Another is selected to sing in the annual Carols by Candlelight televised choir. Another visits Antarctica. Another renovates their backyard. Another publishes a book.

None of these achievements are possible without smart, hard work. When you practise smart, hard work in one element of your life, it becomes easier to practise it at work.

As a result, the organisation benefits. The culture of success spreads across all aspects of life. Imagine the positivity and the success mindset this would create within your organisation!

Various models exist for how this can be achieved:

- You purchase books for your staff and conduct a launch of the program where I will speak and set the scene for the program.
- You purchase access to the online course for your staff.
- You conduct a series of live in-person bootcamps for your staff.
- You conduct a series of live on-line bootcamps for your staff.
- A combination of all of the above.

If you would like to explore how this would work in your organisation, email yesforsuccess@orgsthatmatter.com

ACKNOWLEDGEMENTS

In the journey towards achieving life harmony, success and fulfillment, it is not possible to create a book like this alone. I am deeply grateful to the remarkable individuals whose unwavering support and contributions have made *Yes For Success* a reality. Their dedication reflects the very essence of this book, empowering readers to develop a comprehensive roadmap for personal transformation.

First and foremost, my heartfelt gratitude goes to my incredible wife, Michelle Ryan, and twin brother Denis Ryan; your invaluable feedback and meticulous insights breathed life into the manuscript, ensuring it resonates deeply with our readers. Your unwavering commitment to excellence has been instrumental.

To Louis Salguero, whose exceptional talent and creativity brought our book cover to life. Your artistry sets the tone for the transformative journey within these pages.

Aiden and Darcy Ryan, you both embarked on an extraordinary endeavour during your school holidays, laying the foundation for the initial draft of this manuscript. Your dedication is a source of immense pride.

Amid a bustling performing arts schedule, Callum Ryan demonstrated remarkable dedication by crafting the captivating landing pages that drive the book's promotion and sales. Your efforts exemplify the power of determination.

I extend my heartfelt appreciation to a distinguished group of early readers who not only embraced the book but also graciously shared their testimonials: Prosper Taruvinga, Dean Munro, Maree Harris PhD, Sophie Tversky, Alison Wheeler, and Malcolm Deery. Your words of encouragement provide invaluable guidance to those seeking their own path to success and fulfillment.

To my beloved siblings, Carmel, Sheryl and Alan, your unwavering support on social media has been a beacon of encouragement. Every share has amplified our message, and for that, I am profoundly thankful.

To Gary Micu Jr, Nick Yerhart, Alison Wheeler, Tiffany Everett and Robert Duran, thank you all for holding me to account every Saturday morning at 6:30 a.m. here in Australia. Working with people who understand the importance of accountability for action has played a major role in creating the positive pressure required to complete this project.

Niki Petousis and Teresa Kennedy, your dedication to promoting our work on social media has not gone unnoticed. Your support has been a driving force in spreading the message of *Yes For Success*.

Lastly, to you, the dedicated reader of this book, I extend my sincerest appreciation. Your commitment to crafting your personal plan for life harmony, success and fulfillment is a testament to your unwavering determination. I acknowledge the effort you invest in yourself and wish you boundless success on your journey.

BIBLIOGRAPHY AND RESOURCES

Cardone, G. (2011) *The 10X Rule: The Only Difference Between Success and Failure.* John Wiley & Sons, New Jersey

Chapman, B., & Sisodia, R. (2015) *Everybody Matters – The Extraordinary Power of Caring for Your People Like Family.* Penguin Random House, UK.

Clear, J. (2018) *Atomic Habits: Tiny changes, Remarkable Results. An Easy & proven Way to Build Good Habits & Break Bad Ones.* Random House Business Books, USA.

Cooper, R.K. PhD, (2002) *The Other 90% – How to Unlock Your Vast Untapped Potential for Leadership and Life.* Crown.

Covey, S.R. (1989) *The 7 Habits of Highly Effective People.* Simon and Schuster Ltd, New York.

Covery, S.R., & Merrill, A.R. (1994) *First Things First.* Simon & Schuster Ltd, New York.

Edmondson, A.C. (2019) *The Fearless Organization – Creating Psychological Safety in the Workplace for Learning, Innovation, and Growth.* John Wily & Sons, Hoboken, New Jersey.

Ericcson, K.A., & Poole, R. (2016) *Peak – How All of Us Can Achieve Extraordinary Things.* Penguin Randon House, UK.

Frankl, V.E. (2006) *Man's Search For Meaning.* Beacon Press. USA.

Fritz, R. (1989) *The Path of Least Resistance – Learning to Become the Creative Force in Your Own Life.* Random House, Toronto.

Goldsmith, M., & Reiter, M. (2007) *What Got You Here Won't Get You There – How Successful People Become Even More Successful.* Hyperion. New York.

Hill, N. (1937) *Think and Grow Rich.* The Ralston Society, USA.

Hunt, M. (1998) *Dream Makers – Putting Vision & Values To Work.* Davies Black Publishing, Palo Alto.

Jones, D. (2002) *Celebrate What's Right With The World.* Video program.

Lakhiani, V. (2019) *The Code of The Extraordinary Mind – Ten Unconventional Laws to Redefine Your Life & Succeed On Your Own Terms.* Rodale Books, New York.

Low-Kramen, B. (2023) *Staff Matters – People-Focused Solutions for the Ultimate Workplace.* Ultimate Workplace Press

Pressfield, S. (2015) *Do The Work: Overcome Resistance and Get Out of Your Own Way.* Black Irish Entertainment LLC.

Rock, D. (2020) *Your Brain At Work – Revised and Updated.* Harper Business. New York.

Ryan, G. (2021) *Disruption Leadership Matters: lessons for leaders from the pandemic.* Inspire Publishing, Canberra.

Ryan, G. (2010) *What Really Matters for Young Professionals! How to Master 15 Practices to Accelerate Your Career.* What Really Matters Publishing, Melbourne.

Ryan, G. (2013) *Energy for Success – Seven Steps To Generate The Energy You Need For Success.* eBook. What Really Matters Publishing, Melbourne.

Seligman, M.E.P. (2011) *Learned Optimism: How to Change Your Mind and Your Life.* Random House Australia, Sydney.

Senge, P. (2006) *The Fifth Discipline – The Art & Practice of The Learning Organization.* Revised and Updated Edition. Random House, UK.

Sinek, S. (2011) *Start With Why – How Great Leaders Inspire Everyone To Take Action.* Penguin Random House, UK.

BIBLIOGRAPHY AND RESOURCES

Sinek, S. (2019) *The Infinite Game.* Penguin Randon House, Australia

Wheeler, A. (2022) *Living From The Inside Out – How to Become a Modern Day Wonder Woman.* Dean Publishing, Mt. Macedon.

Websites

Dreammakers.org (Michele Hunt's website)

Mindvalley.com (Vishen Lakhiani's website)

Celebratewhatsright.com (Dewitt Jones' website)

thejobhuntingpodcast.com/podcast (Renata Bernarde *The Job Hunting* podcast)

https://movingbeyondbeinggood.buzzsprout.com (*The Moving Beyond Being Good* podcast)

10% Off the Online Program: Use the Coupon **YESFORSUCCESS** at the checkout to get 10% off the *Yes For Success* Online Course.

https://www.orgsthatmatter.com/product/yfs-online-course/
(Yes For Success Online Course)

https://www.orgsthatmatter.com/product/energy-success/
(Energy For Success eBook)

https://www.orgsthatmatter.com/product/disruption-leadership-matters-ebook/ (Disruption Leadership Matters eBook)

https://www.orgsthatmatter.com/product/disruption-leadership-matters-online-course/
(Disruption Leadership Matters Online Course)

https://www.orgsthatmatter.com/product/really-matters-young-professionals-ebook/
(What Really Matters For Young Professionals! eBook)

https://www.renatabernarde.com/talentpredix (TalentPredix)

ABOUT THE AUTHOR

Gary Ryan is the ninth of eleven children. He and wife, Michelle, are the proud parents of Liam, Sienna, Callum, Aiden and Darcy. In December 2019, Bonti, a beautiful Groodle, joined the family, too ☺!

Gary founded Organisations That Matter in 2007 and has been serving a wide range of organisations, government agencies and universities throughout this period. Gary is passionate about high performance, and the role leaders have in creating a culture that achieves outstanding results, while equally being great for the people in the organisation. He is also passionate about helping people understand the mindset, tools and techniques that can enable so-called 'ordinary' people to live extraordinary lives. The more people living an extraordinary life, the better our world becomes.

Finally, if you are driving in the high country in Victoria or New South Wales, Australia, do not be surprised if you see Gary and his friends riding their motorcycles!

www.ingramcontent.com/pod-product-compliance
Lightning Source LLC
Chambersburg PA
CBHW050312010526
44107CB00055B/2208